CELEBRITY POLITICS

REAL POLITICS IN AMERICA

Series Editor: Paul S. Herrnson, *University of Maryland*

The books in this series bridge the gap between academic scholarship and the popular demand for knowledge about politics. They illustrate empirically supported generalizations from original research and the academic literature using examples taken from the legislative process, executive branch decision making, court rulings, lobbying efforts, election campaigns, political movements, and other areas of American politics. The goal of the series is to convey the best contemporary political science research has to offer in ways that will engage individuals who want to know about real politics in America.

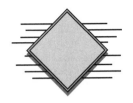

CELEBRITY POLITICS

Darrell M. West
Brown University

John Orman
Fairfield University

UPPER SADDLE RIVER, NEW JERSEY 07458

Library of Congress Control Number: 2002010984

Senior acquisitions editor: Heather Shelstad
Associate editor: Brian Prybella
Editorial assistant: Jessica Drew
Marketing manager: Claire Bitting
Marketing assistant: Jennifer Bryant
Editorial/production supervision: Kari Callaghan Mazzola
Prepress and manufacturing buyer: Ben Smith
Electronic page makeup: Kari Callaghan Mazzola and John P. Mazzola
Interior design: John P. Mazzola
Cover director: Jayne Conte
Cover design: Kiwi Design
Cover photos: photo of Jesse Ventura courtesy of the Minnesota Governor's Office;
    photo of Hillary Rodham Clinton courtesy of the White House Photo Office;
    photo of J. C. Watts, Jr. courtesy of the U.S. Senate

This book was set in 10/12 Palatino by Big Sky Composition
and was printed and bound by Courier Companies, Inc.
The cover was printed by Phoenix Color Corp.

Real Politics in America
Series Editor: Paul S. Herrnson

© 2003 by Darrell M. West and John Orman
Pearson Education, Inc.
Upper Saddle River, New Jersey 07458

Printed in the United States of America
10   9   8   7   6   5   4   3   2   1

ISBN 0-13-094325-8

Pearson Education LTD., London
Pearson Education Australia PTY, Limited, Sydney
Pearson Education Singapore, Pte. Ltd
Pearson Education North Asia Ltd, Hong Kong
Pearson Education Canada, Ltd., Toronto
Pearson Educación de Mexico, S.A. de C.V.
Pearson Education—Japan, Tokyo
Pearson Education Malaysia, Pte. Ltd
Pearson Education, Upper Saddle River, New Jersey

To our Indiana University American government professors:
Marjorie Hershey, Jeff Fishel, James Kuklinski, and Leroy Rieselbach

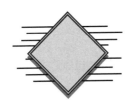

Contents

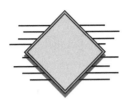

PREFACE

The 2000 election was a presidential election in which the leading candidates were two sons of former politicians (George W. Bush and Al Gore), a former basketball player (Bill Bradley), and a former prisoner of war (John McCain). Hillary Rodham Clinton made history by becoming the only first lady to run for and win a U.S. Senate seat. Four Kennedys (Ted and Patrick Kennedy, Kathleen Kennedy Townsend, and Mark Shriver) now serve in elective office, and a former professional wrestler, Jesse Ventura, is governor of Minnesota. Celebrityhood pervades the political process from campaigns and elections to governing, lobbying, and legislating.

Celebrity Politics looks at the history and contemporary role of celebrities in American politics, and the long-term implications of this trend. It examines the intersection of prominent families such as the Kennedys, Bushes, and Clintons with entertainment figures like Charlton Heston (now head of the National Rifle Association), Warren Beatty, the Rock, and Barbra Streisand. In this book, we analyze the celebrities, from John Glenn and Jim Bunning to Jesse Jackson, Jr., and Steve Largent, who have served in Congress in recent years. Our discussion of governing looks at the Reagan, Bush (both father and son), and Clinton presidencies to see how politicians use celebrities to raise money and issue awareness on a wide variety of causes. We show how television and movies intersect with the political process, as demonstrated by the popularity of the NBC show, "West Wing." Since this book examines celebrity politics in historical context as well as in the contemporary situation, it can be used as a valuable supplementary reading in Introduction to American Politics courses as well as classes on mass media, campaigns and elections, Congress, the presidency, parties, interest groups, and popular culture.

Despite the importance of the subject, few books address celebrity politics. David Canon has a fine book, *Actors, Athletes, and Astronauts*, which looks at the periodic entry of prominent individuals into the U.S. Congress, but it was published more than ten years ago and focuses mainly on House elections. Darrell West is the author of *Patrick Kennedy: The Rise to Power*, which looks at how the next generation of Kennedys is moving to center stage. John Orman talked about the problems of celebrity politics in his book *Presidential Accountability*. A decade ago, journalist Ron Brownstein wrote *The Power and the Glitter*, which looked at the "Hollywood–Washington Connection," while Len Sherman penned *The Good, the Bad and the Famous*, which spotlighted the growing tendency of celebrities to get involved in the political process. The relative paucity of up-to-date materials on the Hollywoodization of politics convinced us that there was a need for a book dealing with this subject.

In the 1990s, the now-defunct magazine *George*, started by the late John F. Kennedy, Jr., demonstrated how all politics had become entertainment and how pop culture had become political. In this era of politics *as* entertainment and entertainment *as* politics, what has become of the political process, and what has become of popular culture? In a time when the deaths of Princess Diana and John F. Kennedy, Jr., are covered around the globe, the distinction between public life and pop culture has virtually disappeared. Celebrities run for political office (or lobby those who do), and operatives such as George Stephanopoulos, Geraldine Ferraro, Oliver North, and Jesse Ventura become celebrated figures. With popular culture merging with the political system, the press has moved toward a style of reporting that emphasizes Hollywood-style gossip and scandal, to the detriment of traditional politicians and political parties.

Critics warn of the deleterious effects that pop culture has on society and politics. Political accountability is undermined. Myths are manufactured in order to boost ratings. Images and stories are made into the commodities of pop culture. Leaders no longer are people in major positions, but rather are famous celebrities who sign autographs. As pointed out by social commentator Leo Braudy, fame has become democratized and no longer is restricted to queens, kings, and popes. Since the turn of the twenty-first century, the signs have been clear that the American political system has changed into a celebrity regime where politicians are subjected to Hollywood-style tabloid coverage and celebrities are treated as political actors. It is all part of the entertaining of America. No longer does the argument of whether pop culture influences political change or vice versa matter. Politics *is* pop culture.

The blurring of sports figures, comedy stars, newscasters, models, movie stars, television performers, rock idols, and politicians has become so dominant that citizens find it difficult to distinguish news from entertainment. Veteran CBS news anchor Dan Rather pointed out in a recent interview that "entertainment values are very close to overwhelming the values of hard news." Elements within pop culture intentionally blur the distinctions between Washington and Hollywood. The media cover pop culture celebrities as interchangeable cogs in the entertainment industry. Activist celebrities themselves have moved into the political process, both as candidates and lobbyists. Citizens legitimize celebrity politics by providing audiences for tabloid news shows and paying attention when personal scandals erupt.

The future of the celebrity political system raises a host of questions: Does the entry of celebrities into the political process represent the best or worst of American politics? Are we doomed to be led by knaves or do celebrities represent a valuable opportunity to reinvigorate the political process by bringing in new blood with innovative ideas? Has celebrity politics trivialized substance and undermined true achievement in our society? This book will try to explain how we got to where we are today, and what it means for our collective fate.

The outline of this book is as follows: Chapter 1 defines the notion of celebrity politics and shows how it has evolved over the course of American history. Chapter 2 shows how the media facilitate the creation of celebrityhood, and Chapter 3 examines the role of money in celebrity politics. Chapter 4 discusses how the advent of television created presidential celebrities. Chapters 5 and 6, respectively, look at activist celebrities and sports politicos. Chapter 7 shows the downside of celebrityhood—comedians who make fun of prominent individuals. Chapter 8 looks at public evaluations of the celebrity regime, and Chapter 9 shows how celebrityhood has transformed American political culture and created serious difficulties for democratic systems.

ACKNOWLEDGMENTS

We would like to thank the following people who, through their writing, helped us formulate our ideas about celebrity politics: Murray Edeleman, Dan Nimmo, James Combs, Carl Bernstein, Michael Parenti, Keith Blume, Ron Brownstein, Norman Corwin, Simon Frith, David Canon, Michael Genovese, Marjorie Hershey, Kathleen Hall Jamieson, Deyan Sudjic, Larry Sabato, Holli Semetko, Paul Slansky, John Street, Bruce Miroff, Thomas Cronin, George Edwards, and Jeff Fishel. Sally Williams and Melissa Driscoll helped us prepare the manuscript, and our families encouraged us to finish the project. Dana Chicchelly did an excellent job of copy editing our manuscript. Series editor Paul Herrnson made a number of helpful comments at various stages of this project. Finally, thanks go to spouses Annie Schmitt and Reenie Demkiw, as well as children Natalie, Katie, and Nicholas Demkiw-Orman.

Darrell M. West

John Orman

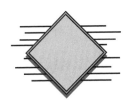

CELEBRITY POLITICS

THE EVOLUTION OF CELEBRITYHOOD

No event better illustrated the intersection of Hollywood and politics than a scene from the 2000 presidential election. Martin Sheen, who plays President Josiah Bartlet on the NBC hit television show *West Wing*, was campaigning for Democratic presidential candidate Al Gore. Appearing at a rally right before the election, Sheen endorsed Gore and encouraged citizens to turn out to vote. The television star then followed the vice president down the rope-line greeting fans. Actor Ben Affleck appeared at the same gathering. Wearing an expensive leather sports coat, on which he had pasted a Gore/Lieberman sticker, Affleck joked, "You gotta sacrifice for the cause. It's a $3,000 Armani, but I'd throw it to the ground and step on it for Al Gore."[1]

Republicans had their own celebrity supporters. Action artist Chuck Norris campaigned for GOP nominee George W. Bush as did actress Bo Derek.[2] World Wrestling Federation star, "the Rock," (also known as Dwayne Johnson) appeared at the Republican convention where he was prominently seated next to Barbara Bush and House Speaker Dennis Hastert. Republican National Committee spokesman Mark Pfeile justified the "smackdown" appeal by noting, "We need to reach out to voters through any means necessary."[3]

Between these and other actions, our political system has been transformed into one dominated by "celebrity politics." If Andy Warhol predicted that in the future everyone would be famous for fifteen minutes, he was mistaken. America's entertaining popular culture just does not have enough space to allow *all* of its citizens to become famous. Besides, the celebrity, the celebrated, the famous, and the hero already monopolize the public sound bite space.[4] These celebrities are loved, hated, admired, despised, chronicled, charted, spied upon, and watched by the media. We cannot aspire to having a political system of philosopher-kings because today we have the "celebrity king and queen" in our star-ladened politics.

As shown in Table 1-1, there are five different types of celebrities: political newsworthies (politicians and handlers skilled at public relations and self-promotion), legacies (children or spouses of former politicians), famed nonpoliticos known in fields outside of politics who run for elective office, famed nonpoliticos who act as lobbyists or issue spokespersons (such as actors, singers, business people, athletes, and astronauts), and event celebrities (individuals such as crime victims who gain notoriety overnight due to some tragedy, event, or life situation). Each differs in important respects from the others in terms of how fame originates and the consequences for our society and culture. Some, such as legacies, present deeper challenges for democratic political systems than do event celebrities.

TABLE 1-1   TYPES OF CELEBRITY POLITICOS

POLITICAL NEWSWORTHIES

James Carville	Mary Matalin
George Stephanopoulos	Jesse Jackson, Sr.
John McCain	Barney Frank

LEGACIES

Patrick and Joe Kennedy	Kathleen Kennedy Townsend
George W. and Jeb Bush	Al Gore
Jay Rockefeller	Jesse Jackson, Jr.
Harold Ford, Jr.	Evan Bayh

FAMED NONPOLITICOS (ELECTED OFFICIALS)

Ronald Reagan	John Glenn
Jim Bunning	Sonny Bono
Jim Ryun	Steve Largent
Jesse Ventura	Jack Kemp
Bill Bradley	J. C. Watts

FAMED NONPOLITICOS (LOBBYISTS AND SPOKESPERSONS)

Charlton Heston	Barbara Streisand
Jane Fonda	Paul Newman/Joanne Woodward
Marlon Brando	Warren Beatty
Robert Redford	Martin Sheen
Willie Nelson	

EVENT CELEBRITIES

Denise Brown	Carolyn McCarthy
Anita Hill	Sarah Brady
Marisleysis Gonzalez	Ryan White

Political newsworthies are the classic celebrities, individuals such as James Carville, Mary Matalin, Jesse Jackson, Sr., and George Stephanopoulos who are skilled at appearing on television and communicating with the general public. In a society that values punchy and entertaining commentary, pundits and leaders earn extensive airtime and become famous for their espousal of particular issues. Carville, for example, guided Clinton to victory in 1992, and then spent the next decade serving as a Democratic attack dog against Republicans. Mary Matalin carved out a visible niche for herself as a GOP advocate for party causes. Jesse Jackson, Sr., is a passionate spokesperson on behalf of minorities and the downtrodden. By articulating prominent concerns and making sly digs at opponents, such people both inform and entertain, and attract large audiences in the process. Jackson even earned his own talk show on CNN.

Legacies include descendants of prominent political families, such as the Kennedys, Rockefellers, Gores, and Bushes. Purely by dint of the family name, these individuals are famous owing to their connection to former politicians. The Bush dynasty now extends over three generations and includes one Senator (Prescott Bush), two presidents (George Herbert Walker Bush and George W. Bush), a vice president (George Herbert Walker Bush), and two governors (George W. and Jeb Bush). With a legacy of public service, famous descendants piggyback on the high name identification and reputation for serving the community of their ancestors.

Fame, of course, does not guarantee political victory, but it is an important asset for these kinds of families. Kathleen Kennedy Townsend lost her first bid for Congress against an incumbent officeholder. Several descendants of the Roosevelt family unsuccessfully sought to convert their famous last name into a political career.

Oftentimes, legacy politicians encounter extensive problems dealing with celebrity status because critics decry their advancement as opportunistic and non-merit-based. For example, when Ted Kennedy first ran for the U.S. Senate in 1962 with one brother in the White House and another serving as Attorney General, an opponent uttered the famous line that if Kennedy's name were Edward Moore and not Edward Moore Kennedy, he would not be taken seriously.[5] The same was true when son Patrick Kennedy ran for Congress in 1994. His opponent complained about citizens voting for a name without much substance to the record. Such ascribed status, rather than demonstrated achievement, clouds the public life of these individuals and invites snide comments about advancement through fame, money, and name alone.

Because their families are well-known, legacies bring all sorts of expectations about the individual based solely on their name. On the negative side, these individuals challenge the democratic norm of fair competition because lineage confers so many advantages in terms of name identification, fundraising, and media coverage. In a democratic nation that prides itself on "one person, one vote," equal opportunity, and upward mobility for those born of humble roots, the political success of famous and wealthy legacies challenges America's self-conception that anybody can grow up to become president.

Yet these kinds of prominent individuals typically have a deeply ingrained sense of public service owing to their family's past civic contributions. Through generations of self-sacrifice, philanthropy, and community work, legacy politicians are well-trusted by voters. Unlike conventional politicians who are forced to cut political deals and sacrifice principles along the path to success, legacies often jump to the front of the line and run for high office without undergoing lengthy political apprenticeships.[6]

In contrast, famed nonpoliticos are responsible for their own prominence. These are people such as John Glenn, Jim Bunning, Ronald Reagan, Jesse Ventura, and Jack Kemp who run for office after becoming famous in another area or individuals such as Charlton Heston, Barbra Streisand, or Jane Fonda who lobby on behalf of social causes. Nonpoliticos piggyback fame in one sector onto political life. In a society that elevates sports stars, entertainers, and astronauts, nonpoliticos are seen as political "white knights." Since their prominence comes from outside the political world, these individuals have a high degree of public trustworthiness and star power to boot.

Unlike legacies, who must deal with a fame that is not of their own doing, famed nonpoliticos generally are confident regarding their own fame and fortune. Because they gained acclaim outside of the political realm, they are used to being in the public spotlight and dealing with the accoutrements of celebrityhood—media coverage, adoring fans, gossip columnists, and intrusions into their private lives. This experience makes their entry into a regime based on celebrity politics easier to handle.

Event celebrities are overnight sensations who arise on the local or national scene due to some tragedy or predicament. Generally, these are individuals who were not politically active or socially prominent. Simply by dint of special circumstances, they generate news coverage and become prominent for their high credibility in speaking out about a particular subject. In a very short period of time, their visibility skyrockets.

Crime victims, relatives of crime victims, or parties to a scandal are prominent examples of this genre. Owing to the tendency of the media to highlight these kinds of stories, crime and scandal (or its allegations) have created a number of famous personalities. Owing to saturation media coverage, people such as Denise Brown (the sister of murder victim Nicole Brown Simpson), Carolyn McCarthy (wife of a man slain during the Long Island Railroad shooting spree who went on to win a New York House seat), Sarah Brady (wife of wounded Reagan Press Secretary James Brady and a prominent gun control spokesperson), and Anita Hill (a witness against the Supreme Court confirmation of Clarence Thomas) have become prominent and are put in a position where they subsequently are able to influence the policy process.

For example, Brown used her notoriety gained during the O. J. Simpson murder trial to become a national spokesperson on domestic violence. From 1994 to 1999, Denise Brown raised around $800,000 for the Nicole Brown Charitable Foundation to help build "transitional housing centers" for battered women. The homes provide shelter for women and children for up to two years, and assist residents in gaining job and parenting skills.[7] She also appeared at Washington press conferences publicizing efforts to toughen domestic violence laws. When Georgia Republican Bob Barr sought to pass legislation exempting law enforcement and military personnel from regulations designed to remove guns from convicted spouse abusers, Brown complained that police groups were seeking a special exemption and noted that, "they think that somehow their domestic violence is OK. Well, it's not OK."[8]

Following the personal tragedy of her husband's shooting, McCarthy became a leading advocate of the need for gun control. She had been a nurse for much of her adult life, but when her husband was killed and son partially paralyzed, McCarthy moved onto the national speaker's circuit. At benefits for Mothers Against Violence in America, she criticized the financial and human costs of gunshot victims. "My son's medical bills have topped $1 million and I know his medical bills will continue because he needs more surgery, more physiotherapy, more everything," she explained. "As a mother, watching him struggle to pick up his son breaks my heart." After the Long Island Railroad shooting of her husband and son in 1993, she ran for Congress in 1996 and was elected. Gun control became her top legislative priority and she had special credibility in addressing that topic given her personal suffering due to gun violence.[9]

Sarah Brady used the tragedy of her husband's shooting and subsequent paralysis in the 1981 assassination attempt on President Ronald Reagan to become an advocate of stricter gun control. Traveling around the country and speaking out against gun violence, Brady built an organization known as Handgun Control that helped raised money for a cause that was of great concern to many Americans. Among her goals was legislation that would require criminal background checks on people purchasing guns at gun shows.[10]

Anita Hill is an example of a person who was not well-known, but became politically prominent through her role in the Clarence Thomas Supreme Court confirmation hearings. A law professor at the University of Oklahoma, Hill erupted onto the national consciousness in 1991 when she accused Thomas of sexual harassment. Years earlier, she had worked for him at the U.S. Equal Employment Opportunity Commission. In Senate hearings televised coast-to-coast, she detailed his constant comments about wanting to date her and explained why harassment was a serious issue in the workplace. Shortly after the hearings, Hill became a hot speaker on the lecture circuit, giving hundreds of talks around the world and publishing a book, *Speaking Truth to Power*, that became a best-seller. Eventually, she was hired as a legal analyst on Court TV. Explaining how she became prominent, she told one reporter, "I did not choose the issue of sexual harassment; it chose me. And having been chosen, I have come to believe that it is up to me to try and give meaning to it all."[11]

Crime, violence, or scandals are not the only ways event celebrities come to prominence. In 1999, six-year-old Elian Gonzalez became a household name when his refugee boat trip from Cuba ended in disaster. His mother and the boat's crew members drowned, and Elian became the sole survivor of that ill-fated boat ride. Immediately embraced by his extended family in Miami, Florida, Gonzalez became to the Cuban-American community in South Florida an international symbol of opposition to Fidel Castro's authoritarian regime in Cuba. However, to friends and family members in Cuba, Gonzalez represented something else, the need to reunite a young boy with his father, Juan Miguel Gonzalez, who remained in Cuba.[12]

For months, the tug-of-war between family members in Miami (such as Lazaro and Marisleysis Gonzalez) and in Cuba continued. Reporters hovered around a modest Miami home as relatives and public officials argued over whether the young boy should be allowed to remain in the United States or be repatriated to his father in Cuba. In April 2000, the Immigration and Naturalization Service moved in, forcibly grabbing the young boy, and handing him over to his father for return to Cuba. Shortly afterwards, Juan Miguel Gonzalez was named a "national hero" in Cuba for his role in protecting the honor of his country in this international episode.[13]

Event celebrities sometimes are created through national tragedies such as the September 11, 2001 terrorist attacks on New York City and Washington, D.C. In the wake of this horrific trauma, New York City police and fire personnel as well as family members of those killed became prominent. For example, Lisa Beamer, wife of Todd Beamer who died on the ill-fated United Flight 93 that crashed in Pennsylvania, appeared on *Larry King Live* and *Good Morning America*. Along with others such as Stephen Push whose wife died on the airplane that hit the Pentagon, and Tom Roger whose daughter was a flight attendant who was killed, family members spoke out on issues from the proper compensation owed to the bereaved to the adequacy of new airport security measures.[14]

Despite clear differences in how star power is gained, each fame category is part of the emerging pattern of celebrity politics that has transformed American politics. Prominent individuals use fame either to run for elective office or influence those who do. They are able to draw on their platform to raise money for themselves and other politicians. In a media-centered political system, celebrities are adept at attracting press attention. They make great copy, and reporters love to build stories around glamorous celebrities.

In a variety of ways, celebrities have become integrally involved in activities such as electioneering, campaigning, fund-raising, endorsing, and lobbying. Their centrality in the mobilization of interests and recruitment of candidates gives them special power. They are able to position themselves in ways that enhance their overall influence. Taken together, these components of celebrity politics make for an eye-grabbing and entertaining American political culture, one that raises a host of important issues for democratic political systems.

In many respects, this trend toward celebrity politics is not new in the United States. Our system has always produced presidents, such as George Washington, Andrew Jackson, and U. S. Grant, who were famous before they entered public service. Washington gained renown as the revolutionary war commander, Jackson was known for fighting Native Americans, and Civil War general Grant was able to ride his celebrity general status to the White House. The Whig Party of the 1840s even captured the American presidency by running a string of famous generals like William Henry Harrison and Zachary Taylor for the nation's top office. In this respect, the nineteenth century was a precursor to twentieth century-generals such as Dwight Eisenhower who became president and military leaders such as George Marshall, Douglas MacArthur, Norman Schwarzkopf, and Colin Powell who gained political prominence.

Other historical leaders were legacy politicians who came from celebrated families like the Roosevelts, the Adams, and the Harrisons. From these three families came six presidents (Theodore and Franklin Roosevelt, John and John Quincy Adams, and William Henry Harrison and Benjamin Harrison). Not only did John Quincy Adams become the first son to become president after his father had served, but also Quincy Adams ran for Congress and won after he left the presidency. In most of these cases, though, the legacy only lasted a generation. Despite the effort of John Quincy Adams and Franklin Roosevelt's kin to run for office, no descendant managed to win high elective office.

Throughout American history, there have been families that achieved great political success across generations. When Blair Lee became governor of Maryland in the 1970s, he was the twenty-first member of his extended family to hold political office at some point since 1647. The Longs of Louisiana, Byrds of Virginia, Talmadges of Georgia, Tafts of Ohio, and Browns of California produced several prominent politicians. According to Stephen Hess, "there have been some 700 families in which two or more members have served in Congress, and they account for 1,700 of the 10,000 men and women who have been elected to the federal legislature since 1774."[15]

America also has seen celebrated nonpoliticos, such as Charles Lindbergh, Mark Twain, Horace Greeley, and Ernest Hemingway, who were politically active. Lindbergh was the first pilot to fly solo, nonstop across the Atlantic and went on to lead the isolationist movement that attempted to keep the United States out of World War II. Twain loved to twit political figures with clever quips and snide jokes, similar to today's late-night comedians. Greeley was one of the foremost newspaper publishers of his day, who helped to elect Abraham Lincoln president. Hemingway was a famous novelist whose nonfiction works covered both domestic and international affairs.

But several trends over recent decades have converged to accelerate this historical tendency toward celebrity politics. The emergence of radio and television, the democratization of fame, and shifts in how journalists perform their craft have altered the dynamics of our culture, and made it possible for celebrities of many different stripes to move into the political system in large numbers. In these respects, then, the contemporary situation is different from past eras and poses greater challenges to a democratic political system.

Radio and then television were perfect media for a celebrity-oriented political system. For the first time in American history, radio offered famous individuals an opportunity to communicate with the general public in ways that were both personal and intimate. Radio's emergence in the 1920s and 1930s made national stars out of people such as Huey Long of Louisiana and Father Charles Coughlin. Television contributed to this trend even more clearly by joining the intimacy of radio with the visual power of television. The latter's emergence in the 1940s and 1950s made a video star out of Dwight Eisenhower by bringing him directly into our living rooms. Indeed, Eisenhower stands out as our first television political superstar. "Ike," as he was known, had been a celebrated World War II hero and college president who used his celebrity status to seek public office. The marriage of Eisenhower the war hero with Eisenhower the television president combined to produce one of the most popular chief executives ever elected.

Television elevated the political fortunes of John F. Kennedy by joining the communications power of the electronic medium with the myth-making power of the "Camelot" years. The media coverage of his extended family and personality made Kennedy a video legend even before his tragic assassination on November 22, 1963. Due to his natural charm and quick wit, Kennedy used his telegenic appeal to great advantage. After his death, the Kennedy myth and legend continued to grow. Brothers Robert and Edward Kennedy continued the family's legacy of public service, and now a new generation of Kennedys (Patrick Kennedy, Kathleen Kennedy Townsend, and Mark Shriver) has won elective office.[16]

Another trend that encouraged celebrity politics has been the "democratization" of fame. As discussed by commentator Leo Braudy, previous epochs in which fame was restricted to royalty, the aristocracy, and those in formal leadership roles gave way to a flowering of celebrityhood in many walks of life.[17] No longer was fame restricted to legacies or individuals holding privileged positions, such as kings and popes, but it was possible for ordinary people to be elevated to social and political prominence.

Event celebrities are the clearest contemporary example of this tendency. Media coverage of unusual life circumstances makes it possible for completely unknown individuals to become *causes célèbres*. For example, horrendous circumstances catapulted a young, hemophiliac boy named Ryan White, who contracted AIDS in 1984 through a transfusion, into fame. Through no misdeed on his own part, White suffered the ignominy of an early death. However, his personal tragedy helped humanize a disease that previously had been stereotyped as a "gay" disease.[18]

The same was true for victims of traumas such as the Columbine school shooting or the bomb explosion that ripped apart the Alfred P. Murrah Federal Building in the middle of Oklahoma City.[19] Simply by the dint of particular circumstances, unknown individuals became national celebrities, at least for a short period of time. Reporters turned to them for first-hand reports of what had transpired during calamitous events.[20]

The celebrity political system has been reinforced by the establishment of "gossip" journalism in which reporters cover the personal lives of politicians. Journalists moved from reporting the "who, what, and where" of civic life to looking at leaders' backgrounds, integrity, and personal foibles. Drinking, womanizing, and drug use became fair game for reporters who sought to determine whether leaders held sufficient character for public office.

Gossip journalism arose during the era of Vietnam and Watergate, when presidents were found to have lied. This led reporters to probe the personal qualities of politicians in order to ascertain whether they could be trusted to perform the basic responsibilities of public office. It became a short hop and skip for reporters to move from examining official government misconduct to the personal behavior of the individuals who either held or sought public office.

Candidates such as Gary Hart, Joe Biden, and Bill Clinton were the objects of extensive press scrutiny. Journalists started to report rumors, hearsay, and background charges regarding personal qualities. Did the politician have affairs, use drugs, or drink too much? If so, what did it indicate about the personal character of the individual? Soon, the lives of politicians were being covered in the breathless manner of Hollywood movie stars. Sensationalized accounts became common, and some politicians didn't make the character cut.

It was not long before the celebrity-star system became institutionalized with politicians becoming interchangeable with other guest celebrities on television talk shows. Politicians emerged as the central dramatic figures on the nightly news drama. American citizens quickly became used to watching politics rather than participating in the system. Voter turnout plummeted during this period, while citizen mistrust rose.

In addition to expressing their views about civic life, celebrities from the Hollywood entertainment industry became elected officials.[21] Actors like Helen Douglas and George Murphy crossed over into the political arena in the late 1940s and early 1950s. A successful Hollywood actress, Douglas ran for the U.S. House in 1944 and won. Six years later, she faced off against Richard Nixon for U.S. Senate. However, this time she was not as effective. Taking advantage of her history as a New Deal Democrat who fought hard for liberal causes, Nixon characterized her as a communist who was "pink right down to her underwear."[22] He won and went on to a long, national career.

Murphy meanwhile gained fame for becoming the first actor to win election to the U.S. Senate. After gaining political experience as the president of the Screen Actors Guild, Murphy ran for the Senate in 1964 and was elected as a Republican. Suspicious of the left wing, he formed the Hollywood Republican Committee to "combat the general belief that all Hollywood actors and writers were left-wing."[23] He was defeated for reelection in 1970.

In 1966, a Hollywood actor and corporate television spokesperson named Ronald Reagan became the Governor of California. Suddenly, a glut of celebrity politicos began to emerge in the political system. Former Buffalo Bills quarterback Jack Kemp was elected to the House and former New York Knicks basketball immortal Bill Bradley was elevated to the U.S. Senate from the state of New Jersey. Astronaut John Glenn became a U.S. Senator from Ohio, Clint Eastwood was chosen mayor of Carmel, California, and to demonstrate the power of celebrity politics, Fred Grandy, "Gopher" from the television show *Love Boat* became an Iowa congressman in 1986.

The "Age of Celebrity," as Kirk Scharfenberg dubbed it, began to flourish.[24] Film and television gave us political activists Paul Newman, Joanne Woodward, Robert Redford, and Ed Asner. The sports industry delivered Jack Kemp, Bill Bradley, Roger Staubach, and Tom McMillan to the political process.[25] Comedy and satire generated names such as Robin Williams, Steve Martin, Billy Crystal, Eddie Murphy, and Gilda Radner who had a particular political view within their comedy. Rock music gave us Bruce Springsteen, Jackson Browne, and John Mellencamp. Legacy politicians included George W. Bush, Al Gore, Jesse Jackson, Jr., Harold Ford, Jr., Patrick Kennedy, Evan Bayh, Hillary Clinton, and Hubert Humphrey, III. Finally, there were all-purpose celebrities like Lee Iacocca, Donald Trump, Jerry Falwell, Jesse Jackson, Geraldine Ferraro, and Oliver North, each skilled at the art of television and image-creation.

Celebrity politics fit the needs of a news media that focused on human features, not detailed substance. According to William Winter, who was one of America's first television news broadcasters in 1950, the Reagan era was a time when the news business gave broadcasts that were "increasingly shallow and trivial."[26] Winter noted that "news anchors are usually hare-brained performers whose sole function is to read the TelePrompTer pleasantly. With a public educated by TV news, no wonder they elected Ronald Reagan.[27] He was a superb 'anchor.'" American politics came to be dominated by the nine-second sound bite (later cut to five seconds). The competition in American politics centered around who could produce the best sound bite from the best pseudo-event of the day.

After Reagan's victories in 1980 and 1984, and especially after George Bush's presidential victory in 1988, the importance of consultants, joke writers, speech writers, pollsters, image advisors, ad makers, spin doctors, sound bite writers and delivery coaches in America became institutionalized. Their monopoly of American politics became so great that *Harper's* magazine in April 1989, asked these movers and shakers to plan *the* campaign for the return of the greatest celebrity of them all, Jesus Christ.

Ron Suskind wrote a memo outlining the media schedule and strategy for Jesus Christ's tour of the United States. Al Franken wrote Christ's obligatory monologue for his spot on *Saturday Night Live* as guest host. Gerry Howard, an editor at Norton, designed the jacket flap copy for the new testament and Adelle Lutz, a costume designer, designed the outfits for Jesus Christ's American tour complete with a robe for stadium dates and motorcades. Phyllis Robinson created the television commercials to announce the return of Jesus Christ.[28] The whole project would have been hilarious except that America had become the Celebrity Society and the efforts suggested to market the return of Jesus Christ are the same values needed in promoting rock groups, presidential candidates, books, movies, television shows, comedy performers, or businessmen.[29]

In 1998, former professional wrestler Jesse Ventura shocked the political establishment by capturing the governorship of Minnesota as a "dark horse" independent candidate. Featuring frank talk and folksy good humor, Ventura ran against two better-known candidates, legacy Hubert Humphrey, III, and Norm Coleman, and garnered 37 percent of the three-way vote. Ventura had gained fame by being a star in the World Wrestling Federation, hosting his own radio talk show, and winning election as mayor of a suburban Minneapolis community.

Typical of famed nonpoliticos, he had great credibility with a public (especially young people) that mistrusted conventional politicians. Using antiestablishment ads and shining in campaign debates, Ventura demonstrated that sports politicos could transfer fame to the political process. His media advisor Bill Hillsman explained Ventura's appeal this way: "Jesse's worked in movies, he's been a pro-wrestler, he understands pop culture. He gets it. He knows what's going to play in public, and he's not afraid to take chances."[30]

Following his ascension to the governorship, though, Ventura constantly got into trouble over unconventional or inflammatory comments he made. Since taking office, he "has written about visiting a prostitute in his youth, . . . suggested that lives could have been saved in the Columbine massacre if someone at the school had had a concealed weapon, . . . called organized religion a 'sham' and joked that if reincarnated, he would want to come back as a size-38DD bra, . . . [and] signed on as an NBC analyst for the XFL, a new football league that trumpets violent play and promotes it with risqué ads."[31]

In 2000, celebrities George W. Bush won the presidency and Hillary Clinton was elected to the U.S. Senate from New York. It was the culmination of a media-dominated political system, the high cost of campaigning, and the particular credibility that legacies and nonpoliticians have with the general public. The ties between Washington and Hollywood became so intertwined that a sitting Secretary of State, Madeleine Albright, lobbied producers of the television show *West Wing* to add a character to the show playing a Secretary of State.[32]

As Daniel Boorstin observed in his enlightening book, *The Image*, celebrities and politicians are especially adept at political image-making. He writes in a prescient way: "Tempted like no generation before us, to believe we can fabricate our experience—our news, our celebrities, our adventures, and our art forms—we finally believe we can make the very yardstick by which all these are to be measured. That we can make our very ideals. This is the climax of our extravagant expectations. It is expressed in a universal shift in our American way of speaking: from talk about 'ideals' to talk about 'images.'"[33]

It is not so much that Americans have not had heroes, but during the past few decades, American heroes came to be replaced by "mere celebrities."[34] Politicians no longer are heroes, but are treated and reported on like celebrities. Ever since the Watergate investigative journalism of Woodward/Bernstein in the *Washington Post* during 1972 and 1973, the stories about American politicians lend themselves to *People Magazine*, newsmaker, periscope type of reporting. Celebrity profiles, inside interviews, loss of privacy, scandal creation, and tabloid journalism have characterized reporting about American politics. The personal trials and tribulations of Wilbur Mills, Wayne Hays, Barney Frank, and Dan Quayle have proliferated in the mainstream press.

The celebrity politician has to deal with the new political environment and the demands of celebrityhood. In 1988 when actress Jane Fonda was being hounded by conservatives when filming in Naugatuck, Connecticut, because of her anti–Vietnam War days, she quickly went on Barbara Walters *20/20* news magazine and apologized for some of her actions during the Vietnam protest years.[35] She still had not become the new Jane Fonda to some conservatives. She wasn't Jane Fonda the actress or Jane Fonda the aerobics guru, but rather Hanoi Jane. However, her celebrity platform and ability to command national television helped Fonda survive these protests and put a new spin on her public image.

In the celebrity political system, it helped to have a prominent person backing your cause. In order to get more coverage for their cause, female Vietnam veteran nurses used Loretta Swit (known as "Hot Lips Houlihan" on the TV show *MASH*) to make a tearful plea to win approval for a memorial to women who served in Vietnam.[36] At a hearing on the plight of American farmers in the 1980s, the lead-off witnesses on Capitol Hill were Jane Fonda, Jessica Lange, and Sissy Spacek, three famous actresses who had played farm women in movies in the 1980s. The chair of the House committee, Representative Tom Daschle, defended the hearing by saying the film stars "did not pretend to be farm experts," but were just trying to "educate America."[37] As television cameras captured the footage, Lange "choked back tears" as she bemoaned the plight of farmers. "It is heartbreaking to witness their anguish as they watch their lives being stripped away," she cried.[38]

Now, celebrities are saving everything from farms and rain forests to the Earth itself. On April 22, 1990, Time Warner presented "The Earth Day Special" to save the world from environmental destruction. It was billed as "A day of hope. A night of laughter, music, and celebration." It was "a world event. A world of stars. A world at stake." Scheduled to appear on the ABC television show were: Candice Bergen, Bill Cosby, Kevin Costner, Ted Danson, Meryl Streep, Dustin Hoffman, and a host of other celebrities.

Writer Mickey Kaus dubbed this new form of social activism in which celebrities take public stands on Central America, AIDs, the environment, the rain forest, farm plight, and nuclear weapons as *celebritics*. Kaus observed that in regular politics a candidate might want to seek a celebrity endorsement but, in celebritics, the celebrities become "so powerful that they frame the issues and run the campaign themselves, dispensing with the boring old politicians altogether."[39]

This trend toward politicians using celebrities and celebrities becoming politicians has been encouraged by structural changes in the American media. Media came to be dominated by "infotainment" shows such as *People Magazine*, *US Today*, *Inside Edition*, and *Entertainment Tonight*. Such episodes reported that celebrities were really interesting political people and that politicians had many hidden stories just like other famous people in celebrity gossip. While at CBS, Bill Moyers told of meetings where the *ET* model was promoted. This paradigm was "breezy, entertaining, and undemanding."[40]

The media report the comings and goings of American celebrities as they are tied into the political parties. Both parties have celebrity coordinators and press people who try to coordinate celebrities so that publications like *USA Today* and *People Magazine*, along with the television media, will report celebrity movements at the convention or along the campaign trail.

With the entry of celebrities into American politics, politicians and celebrities become indistinguishable. Politicians regularly appear on American talk shows and in situation comedies, dramas, and variety shows. Among the politicos to have appeared on *Saturday Night Live* are Jesse Jackson, George McGovern, Ed Koch, Daniel Moynihan, and Jesse Ventura. Nancy Reagan did an episode of *Different Strokes* and Gerald Ford and Betty Ford showed up on *Dynasty*. Even the staid Henry Kissinger appeared on *Dynasty* and television news people like Connie Chung and Kathleen Sullivan showed up on *Murphy Brown*.

As Barbara Goldsmith has observed, "Today we are faced with a vast confusing jumble of celebrities: the talented and the untalented, heroes and villains, people of accomplishment and those who have accomplished nothing at all."[41] We are not very discerning as a society when it comes to making qualifications for those to be celebrated. We celebrate almost anyone for any reason. Anyone can be a celebrity if the right breaks happen and, hence, anyone can become a celebrity politico. The problem that this influx of celebrities has on the system is that according to Victoria Sackett, "The public has learned to take politics less seriously and stars more seriously. Politics is the perfect meeting ground. Once a field that was restricted to the able and trained, it is now open to anyone with an opinion and a presence."[42]

Everyone knows that celebrities are citizens and that they have First Amendment freedoms of political expression, but the new celebrity politics has moved well beyond that. Celebrities have important opinions because the media have deemed them to be important celebrities and pronounced their views on issues to be important. The American mass media became the tool that legitimates celebrities' political opinion. It is the increasing coverage of celebrity and politics by the media that makes this American trend all the more important, and which drives out expert opinion and in-depth analysis.

By the last decade, citizens were caught in the state of watching the star-dominated celebrity political system. Voters no longer wished to participate in the political system, but much like Chance, the gardener in the film *Being There*, were content just to watch. The quality of political debate became trivialized and voting participation dropped to all-time lows for the world's greatest democracy. The gossip quotient increased and the entertainment from the news and politics evolved into a 24-hour activity. The attention span for important stories lessened to one- and two-day media cycles. Crisis stories appeared on the television screens like comets competing for public attentiveness. The system that had produced a Washington and a Lincoln was reduced to a political infotainment show dominated by celebrity scandals.

NOTES

1. *Providence Journal*, "Hollywood Sets Stage for Campaign Finale," 2 November 2000, p. A-2.
2. *St. Petersburg Times*, "Celebs Rally Behind Their Presidential Picks," 6 November 2000, p. 2-B.
3. Michael O'Keeffe, "WWF: We'll Rock the Vote This Year," *New York Daily News*, 5 November 2000, p. 95.
4. David Marshall, *Celebrity and Power: Fame in Contemporary Culture* (Minneapolis, MN: University of Minnesota Press, 1997).
5. Burton Hersh, *The Education of Edward Kennedy* (New York: Morrow, 1972).
6. Darrell M. West, *Patrick Kennedy: The Rise to Power* (Englewood Cliffs, NJ: Prentice Hall, 2000).
7. H. G. Reza, "The Brown Foundation Cuts Back on Giving," *Los Angeles Times*, 4 November 1999, p. B-1.
8. Mark Sherman, "Law Taking Guns from Domestic Abusers to Be Tested," *Atlanta Journal*, 2 March 1997, p. 17-A.
9. Sara Jean Green, "Health Costs of Gun Toll Cited," *Seattle Times*, 24 May 2000, p. B-1.

10. *Denver Post*, "Pro- Anti-Gun Groups Take Aim at 6th Congressional District Race," 28 October 2000, p. A-14.
11. Georgia Pabst, "Anita Hill to Speak Tuesday in Lecture Series," *Milwaukee Journal Sentinel*, 28 May 2000, p. 3-B.
12. *Miami Herald*, "New Facts Surface in Elian Affair," 11 January 2001.
13. *Miami Herald*, "Elian's Father Decorated as National Hero in Cuba," 6 July 2000.
14. Jim Rutenberg, "A Handful of the Bereaved Become Advocates for All," *New York Times*, 29 December 2001, p. B-1.
15. Stephen Hess, "Political Dynasties: An American Tradition," www.tompaine.com, February 27, 2000.
16. Darrell M. West, *Patrick Kennedy: The Rise to Power* (Englewood Cliffs, NJ: Prentice Hall, 2000).
17. Leo Braudy, *The Frenzy of Renown: Fame and its History* (New York: Vintage Books, 1986).
18. *New York Times*, "14-Year-Old Boy with AIDS Attends School after 2 Years," 26 August 1986, p. B-3.
19. Paul Queary, "Grand Jury Begins Oklahoma City Bombing," *Associated Press*, 15 July 1997.
20. Lisa Ryckman and Mike Anton, "Mundane Gave Way to Mundane," *Rocky Mountain News*, 25 April 1999.
21. Ronald Brownstein, *The Power and the Glitter: The Hollywood–Washington Connection* (New York: Pantheon Books, 1990).
22. Helen Gahagan Douglas, *A Full Life: Helen Gahagan Douglas* (Garden City, NY: Doubleday, 1982).
23. Kenneth Reich, "From Fame to Shame," *The Guardian*, 8 May 1992, p. 35.
24. Kirk Scharfenberg, "Populism in the Age of Celebrity," *Atlantic Monthly*, June 1990, p. 117.
25. David Canon, *Actors, Athletes, and Astronauts* (Chicago: University of Chicago Press, 1990).
26. Quoted in Ron Miller, "TV News: Increasingly Shallow, Trivial," *Bridgeport Post*, 17 May 1990, p. D-8.
27. Mark Hertsgaard, *On Bended Knee: The Press and the Reagan Presidency* (New York: Farrar, Straus, Giroux, 1988).
28. "He's Back!!!" *Harper's Magazine*, April 1989, pp. 47–55.
29. Joshua Gamson, *Claims to Fame: Celebrity in Contemporary America* (Berkeley: University of California Press, 1994).
30. *Minneapolis Star Tribune*, "This Odd Election: What Will It Mean for Minnesota?" 4 November 1998, p. 28-A and Patricia Lopez Baden, "This Candidate Knew How to Market Himself," *Minneapolis Star Tribune*, 5 November 1998, p. 20-A.
31. *Providence Journal*, "Ventura Not Amused by New Comic Strip," 28 January 2001, p. A-20.
32. Joan Ryan, "It's a Washington–Hollywood Lovefest," *San Francisco Chronicle*, 15 August 2000, p. A-25.
33. Daniel Boorstin, *The Image* (New York: Harper & Row, 1964), p. 181.
34. Dan Hurley, "The End of Celebrity," *Psychology Today*, December 1988, p. 50.
35. Associated Press, "Fonda, Vets Meet in Naugatuck," *Bridgeport Post*, 19 June 1988, p. 50.
36. Desda Moss, "A Plea for War's Healers," *USA Today*, 22 June 1988, p. 4-A.

37. Victoria Sackett, "Stage Craft as Statecraft: Actors' and Politicians' New Roles," *Public Opinion* (May/June 1987), p. 16.
38. Lois Romano, "Fonda, Lange & Spacek Draw a Crowd on the Hill," *Washington Post*, 7 May 1985, p. B-1.
39. Mickey Kaus, "Age of Celebrities," *New Republic*, 24 February 1986, p. 15.
40. Bill Moyers, "Taking CBS News to Task," *Newsweek*, 15 September 1986, p. 53.
41. Barbara Goldsmith, "The Meaning of Celebrity," *New York Times Magazine*, 4 December 1983, p. 75.
42. Victoria Sackett, "Stage Craft as Statecraft: Actors' and Politicians' New Roles," *Public Opinion* (May/June 1987), p. 16.

MEDIA IMAGE-MAKERS

Celebrities are products of the image-making industry that tries to make people famous. For Boorstin, a celebrity was the human equivalent of a "pseudo-event," someone who warranted attention solely for the purpose of being covered. Celebrities are people known for their "well-knownness."[1] The star is the central player in the modern institution known as "the cult of celebrities."[2] This system is built around the personalities of people from the political, television, news, film, comedy, rock, sports, entertainment, business, and newsmakers arenas. Such individuals have been glorified by people who have the job of building fame. Celebrities have become the stars of our "public drama."[3]

Our celebrity political system is dictated by the interaction between politicians, media, and the public. There have been a number of changes in the structure and operation of the American mass media that have facilitated the emergence of celebrity politicians from legacies to event celebrities. Technological developments have led to a proliferation of cable channels, talk shows, Internet sites, and television networks. Simply because there is a much larger number of channels today, 75 to 100 on most cable systems compared to a dozen viewing options three decades ago, it is possible for larger and larger numbers of people to gain social and political prominence through the media. This democratizes fame and illustrates how television has facilitated the creation of celebrity politicians.

Soon, there may be up to 500 channels on digital cable systems. With the drop in barriers to entry to news and entertainment dissemination through talk shows and the Internet, those who are inclined can be on television. The development of 24-hour news networks such as MSNBC, CNN, and C-SPAN provides a forum for political noteworthies, legacies, famed nonpoliticos, and event celebrities to flourish. Even ordinary people, such as Richard Hatch, the first star of the hit CBS television show *Survivor*, can be thrust into stardom with the advent of reality-based shows featuring ordinary people engaging in daily life.[4]

The good old days when a prestige press composed of the *New York Times*, the *Washington Post*, ABC, CBS, NBC, and the wire services dominated civic life has given way to the decline of the media establishment and the rise of alternative viewing options.[5] During the evening news, for example, the networks no longer compete with one another, but with reruns of situation comedies, *Star Trek*, and game shows. Viewers armed with remote control channel changers switch quickly to the next channel if the show does not grab their attention. The core media now compete with the periphery, and news stories can be broken as easily by Internet sites as network television shows.

Witness who broke leading stories over the past decade. Clinton's sex scandal with Monica Lewinsky was first publicized by Internet broadcaster Matt Drudge. The *National Enquirer* printed the story of Jesse Jackson fathering a child out of wedlock with a woman who worked for him. The Web site, Salon.com, was the first news outlet to report during the impeachment hearings that House Judiciary Committee chairperson Henry Hyde had engaged in an adulterous affair with an older woman several decades ago.

These are not isolated examples but illustrations of how dramatically the old media establishment has lost its ability to scoop the competition. Now anybody with a Web site or an unnamed source can make news and influence the manner in which public figures get covered. The previous era when top media figures broke the news and dictated how top stories were reported is over and has been replaced by a Wild West of news coverage.

The economic pressures unleashed by the hypercompetitiveness of the contemporary American media have altered the manner in which all reporters—whether they work for tabloid or mainstream organizations—cover the news. Journalists increasingly cover gossip in order to build audience share. Hard news has been replaced by soft features, scandal, and infotainment. The tabloid press relies on anonymous sources and innuendo to gain provocative information about public figures. These stories then get picked up by mainstream outlets without much additional sourcing. In this media system, the line between Hollywood and Washington has virtually disappeared as politicians are covered as scandal-plagued celebrities.

The changes in our media system have been so dramatic that presidents today have formed "quick response units" and "war rooms" to combat media reporting of personal scandals. The Clinton administration, for example, excelled in the art of spin control. It flooded reporters with information when scandals broke in order to dispel the notion that it was hiding something. Rather than having material dribble out and turn a one-day story into a five-day drama, presidential flacks sought to beat reporters at their own game.[6]

An examination of changes in our political process over the past few decades shows how dramatically the media have become crucial definers of candidate fortunes and how many of these judgments center on background, scandal, and gossip.[7] Before the primaries have even started, reporters winnow the field by informing citizens that some candidates are front-runners, while others are losers, and that some fall short on key dimensions.

As the central gatekeepers, media figures tell political action committees, presidential observers, and opinion leaders how certain candidates are doing on various measures. Fund-raising, for example, has emerged as a crucial standard given the high costs of politicking. One of George W. Bush's top credentials in the eyes of reporters during the two years leading up to the 2000 election was his huge war chest. When his campaign committee reported in 1999 that it had raised $60 million, thereby dwarfing all available rivals, it immediately propelled him to front-runner status.

As pointed out in the next chapter, this emphasis on money by reporters provides celebrities (especially legacy candidates or famed nonpoliticos) with important advantages. The fund-raising standard benefits these types of celebrities because they typically have great personal wealth, owing to family connections or nonpolitical pursuits, or have access to rich supporters who are willing to fund their public ventures.

At other times, candidates have been weakened because they have violated subjective journalistic judgments. For example, George Romney, then Republican governor of Michigan, lost his presidential bid in 1967 when the media attacked him for saying that he had been "brainwashed" by the generals on how the war in Vietnam was going. This was interpreted by reporters as demonstrating that Romney was out-of-touch or delusional in some respect. They concluded he lacked the psychological demeanor to function as president.

In reality, his comments were accurate. As Americans later found out, generals were withholding information and doctoring material to make the Vietnam war effort look more successful that it actually was. A series of investigative pieces by leading journalists demonstrated that the Pentagon was playing fast and loose with the truth. But major media in 1967 concluded that Romney had made a serious mistake in his choice of words and therefore was no longer a serious candidate. This effectively doomed Romney's candidacy.

During 1969, Senator Edward Kennedy was criticized for a car accident in which he drove off a narrow bridge on Chappaquidick Island, and a young female passenger, Mary Jo Kopechne, drowned. Kennedy's lack of forthrightness in discussing the event led to years of negative stories and books about his behavior. Armed with public opinion polls showing grave public doubts, reporters concluded that the Massachusetts senator was damaged goods. This perception doomed Kennedy's 1980 race for the presidency against incumbent Jimmy Carter.[8]

In 1987, the leading contender for the Democratic nomination, Gary Hart, was eliminated from the race because the *Miami Herald* decided to spy on Hart to see if he was having an affair. This was the first time reporters had staked out a candidate to see if he was engaging in adultery. Following widespread rumors that Hart was a philanderer, the stakeout found Hart leaving an apartment with a young woman named Donna Rice with whom he apparently had spent the night.

Media rushed to inform citizens of the result of the investigative search into the candidate's bedroom. Hart at first insisted that reporters had no right to question him about his "private life," but the ensuing clamor became so loud that Hart was unable to discuss anything else. His promising campaign became a national joke and he was forced to withdraw from the race.[9]

The result, according to author Larry Sabato, has been that politics has turned into a "peep show" marred by "feeding frenzies." Noting the changes that have bedeviled the media industry, Sabato points out that "the line political reporters draw between private and public life is perhaps more blurry than ever before. With increasing regularity, that blurry line is the smudged chalk outline of an ambitious politician."[10]

Before the primary season, the media supply trial survey contests, make odds, discuss fund-raising abilities, and occasionally outline issue stands of candidates. This kind of early horse-race journalism shapes the opportunities available to challengers, and encourages celebrity politicians to run for public office.[11] They typically are the types of candidates who score well in early surveys owing to their high name identification and who are able to raise large sums of campaign funds. If political watchers hype a particular candidate, that person's money, support, and news coverage rises dramatically, and it creates a self-fulfilling prophecy in favor of that particular campaigner.

Examples of this occurred when Patrick Kennedy, the son of U.S. senator Ted Kennedy, ran for public office. Elected as a state representative in 1988, Kennedy used the family name to build an image as a clean and trustworthy reformer. In that year, he had toppled an incumbent legislator on primary day by bringing in famous relatives for Polaroid pictures with voters at the polling place. Rather than pass out campaign literature, he gave voters a picture of themselves with celebrities such as John F. Kennedy, Jr. and Joe Kennedy. These photo ops boosted turnout and helped insure an upset victory over Kennedy's opponent.

After six years in the state legislature, Kennedy brought out all the star appeal to win his seat in the U.S. House. Featuring famous Kennedy cousins (such as Joe Kennedy and John F. Kennedy, Jr.), celebrity fund-raisers, and sympathetic press coverage, Kennedy discouraged other strong candidates from running in the Democratic primary and was able to keep the party-nominating field to himself. He then beat a young Republican doctor who never had run for public office before in the general election, and was clearly undermatched in terms of political experience.[12]

Another example of celebrity hyping by the media came in the case of John McCain's 2000 presidential bid. A former prisoner of war during the Vietnam War, McCain had a compelling personal story that attracted a swarm of media coverage. After McCain became "hot," everyone wanted access to him. The resulting favorable press reporting propelled McCain into the top two among the Republican field, although he ultimately lost the nomination to George W. Bush.[13] McCain went on to become the major national spokesperson concerning the need for campaign finance reform.

In an era of celebrity politics, media are too informative about personal themes and horse-race coverage, and not informative enough about substantive issues. It is common for journalists to cover politics in the style of "sports reporters." Americans like to watch politics much the way they do professional sports and entertainment shows. Reporters tell citizens the score and give crucial commentary directed at the leading candidates. The game, strategy, and horse race become the major things that get covered.

During the critical period from Iowa to New Hampshire in the nominating process, mass media have their greatest impact in picking nominees for the major parties. Some have argued that parties do not select the presidential nominees, but that this task has been entrusted to major media. It is evident that huge amounts of poor press accumulating for weeks destroy perceptions and expectations about a candidate. Moreover, it is also the case that big quantities of good press over weeks of accumulation help a candidate. In the end, journalists play a tremendous role in framing the contest and shaping the ultimate choices of voters.

Reporters also are crucial in setting the campaign agenda. The media's agenda setting function has long been observed. Journalists inform citizens about which issues are important enough for discussion.[14] The media uses its special abilities to determine "news."[15] The broadcast media has different news values than print media so the audience hears about different political happenings on television that may not be covered in newspapers with the same emphasis.

Again, these are changes that advantage celebrities. Television news is guided by visual elements and entertainment values.[16] Sometimes this might include information about policy differences between politicians, such as occurred with John McCain's "Straight Talk Express," whereby reporters could directly travel with and question the Republican presidential candidate. The media loved the close access to the campaigner and wrote flattering stories about McCain's life journey as a former Vietnam prisoner of war.

But understanding public policy matters is not the driving focus of televised media. Instead, good copy is, and writing stories that entertain readers is of paramount importance. Candidates often appear with celebrities from outside of politics in order to boost the newsworthiness of their events. In 1980, for example, presidential candidate Jerry Brown campaigned with rock star Linda Ronstadt, who also was his girlfriend at the time. Afterwards, more people at the rally would swarm around her than him in an effort to get her autograph.[17]

Human-feature aspects of particular campaigners are highlighted by reporters. Print media cover politics more in-depth than television because the electronic medium is driven by time constraints, picture needs, and sound-bite demands. Yet even press coverage is constrained by space allotments and the needs of corporate managers to hold costs down amidst the diminishing readership of major American newspapers.

In the early months on the campaign trail, newspapers and television devote much effort to sifting out the poor candidates at the same time they try to construct the image of the front-runner. As soon as leaders are created, media try to create a race that is as close as possible by announcing that the front-runner does not have the nomination sewed up. Reporters feel that they must make the campaign story as sensational, interesting, and dramatic as possible. This projected competition enables media to build interest in the entire presidential selection process. To enhance competition in the minds of the citizenry, journalists announce that the leader has serious flaws and that the closest challengers have exceptional qualities that make them worthy of consideration.

During the 2000 presidential nominating battle, for example, George W. Bush was first lionized as a legacy candidate with broad name identification and strong fund-raising appeal. However, later when reporters grew tired of this narrative, he was portrayed as an empty suit who was campaigning only on the basis of his father's name.[18] That, of course, is the ultimate insult that can be made against any legacy politician.

The attention span for many American citizens during election campaigns is probably two or three days at best for any particular story. Consultants, advisors, media relations, and public relations experts attempt to create favorable images for citizens who tune in to political events.[19] In media and pseudo-events, specialists try to create the ideas of honesty, composure, competency, compassion, toughness, and likability for their candidates. However, specialists do not have the last say with respect to image-making since the media filter campaign presentations. Candidates work very hard to make sure the image of them presented in the mass media reverberates to their political advantage.

Although in the 1988 presidential primary season there were a number of important issues, citizens were told about Gary Hart's extramarital affairs and Joe Biden's problems in terms of personal integrity. People found out that Michael Dukakis was frugal and the architect of the "Massachusetts miracle." Paul Simon from Illinois wore a bow tie, and he was not the same Paul Simon who recorded *Graceland*. Watchers heard about Al Gore's "southern strategy," but they heard more about his wife, Tipper, and her efforts to get record companies to provide voluntary warning labels about content of rock lyrics. Dick Gephardt's eyebrows were too light, and Pat Schroeder never should have cried when she took herself out of the race for president. Wisdom-bearers were shocked when Jesse Jackson did "better than expected" when he concentrated on issues like drugs, jobs, peace, education, and equality. Bruce Babbitt was hardly mentioned despite being one of the most articulate candidates in the race.

The experts indicated that the Republicans had no Ronald Reagans running in 1988, Pat Robertson was a minister, and Al Haig had far too big of an ego. Jack Kemp had played professional football, and he talked incessantly about economics. Bob Dole still had his "mean streak," but he was married to Elizabeth Dole. Pete du Pont was a grown-up, rich preppie, and George Bush was a "wimp."

After Dukakis and Bush secured their party's nomination, the media turned to the question of who would be on each party's ticket at the vice-presidential level. We were informed that Lloyd Bentsen had new-found integrity, and that the Democratic party still had to determine just what did Jesse Jackson really want.

The media went into Eagletonian overkill after Dan Quayle was nominated by George Bush to be his running mate. "Why didn't Quayle serve in Vietnam?" seemed to be the attitude of many reporters. Bush's speechwriters called it a "feeding frenzy" as the media scrambled to tell tales of efforts made on behalf of Quayle to get him into the exclusive Indiana National Guard during the Vietnam War. Had he used special political connections to get out of Vietnam duty, reporters wanted to know? The thrust of many of these stories was that Quayle had gotten preferential treatment and therefore had gained an advantage over his contemporaries.

In the general election, mass media become the theater where the entire national presidential election campaign is acted out. Many items that citizens know about the remaining presidential candidates are gleaned from mass-media presentations. Media dominate the electoral cycle and behave like a national unifying mechanism for the country in terms of information flow.

In the 1988 autumn campaign for president, viewers found out that Boston Harbor was polluted, Dukakis would never force school children to say the "Pledge of Allegiance," and Willie Horton never should have been let out of jail. Media consensus soon became that former "wimp" George Bush was a great campaigner and a strong forceful leader for change. Dukakis, it was reported by all, was too unemotional and boring. In fact, media reminded citizens over and over that Bush had the election locked up and Dukakis was a quintessential loser.

Voters were not informed of the Housing and Urban Development scandal, or about Savings and Loan failures during the Reagan administration. The media did not tell citizens the extent of Bush's involvement with the Iran–Contra scandal or with Manuel Noriega, the dictator of Panama. The problems of trillions of dollars in national debt attracted little attention because the media focused on personality characteristics.

This excessive personalistic media coverage in the 1988 campaign was supposed to have ended that year, but presidential elections of the past decade brought forth new lows in campaign coverage. From the tabloid journalism of the national networks to the celebrity-personality reporting of the major pack journalists on the presidential campaign, the 1992 election was celebrity-driven. That contest featured extensive press attention to the presidential campaign of pundit Pat Buchanan, Bill Clinton's affair with Gennifer Flowers, Ross Perot's appearances on *Larry King Live*, Arsenio Hall, televised phone-in shows, the presidential debate mini-series, and many other entertaining plot lines.

The celebrity character of the 1992 election cycle was demonstrated early through the nomination challenge of CNN pundit Pat Buchanan to sitting president George Bush. Buchanan was famous for being one of the most recognizable celebrity journalists on television. He appeared on *The McLaughlin Group*, *The Capitol Gang*, and other shows, but was most infamous as the conservative voice on CNN's *Crossfire*. He was the conservative pit bull of the national airwaves.[20]

In the celebrity politics era, Buchanan's announcement that he was running for the Republican nomination did not strike anyone as odd even though he had never run for elective office before. The national news media picked up the Buchanan story and treated him as a legitimate challenger. Perhaps he received such glowing coverage because the media wanted to project and cover a dramatic presidential contest. More likely, he generated favorable coverage because he was being covered by his friends inside the Washington, D.C. Beltway.[21]

Regardless of the reason, Buchanan received extraordinary coverage for being a celebrity candidate running for his first national office. Buchanan made outrageous sound-bite comments about gays, AIDS, Jews, and others, but had an aura of respectability. When he failed to win the New Hampshire primary against Bush, the presidential writers argued that Buchanan did "better than expected" and his 37 percent support in one of the most conservative Republican states in America meant serious trouble for Bush.

On the Democratic side, the race started with Bill Clinton, the governor of Arkansas; Senator Bob Kerrey from Nebraska; Senator Tom Harkin from Iowa; former governor of California Jerry Brown; and former senator from Massachusetts, Paul Tsongas. Shortly before the New Hampshire primary, the American media returned to its previous tendency of shallow, tabloid, gossip, shameless journalism. A supermarket tabloid, the *Star*, paid Gennifer Flowers thousands to tell her story that she had been Governor Bill Clinton's extramarital love interest in Arkansas during the 1980s. They broke the story and then flew Flowers to New York to hold her first national press conference on the allegations.

At Flowers' national press conference, reporters probed into her love life. One person, "Stuttering John" of Howard Stern's New York radio show, got in two questions that demonstrated how low the coverage had sunk: "Did Governor Clinton use a condom?" and "Will you be sleeping with any other presidential candidates during this election year?" Flowers acted embarrassed and refused to go on with the press conference if there were any other questions that attacked her "dignity." Thus, Clinton's "character" became the new campaign issue. Even after Clinton wrapped up the nomination, media questions centered on Clinton's persistent efforts to avoid military service during the war in Vietnam and whether he had smoked marijuana. Comedian Jay Leno joked that you know you have a bad war record when your record makes Dan Quayle look like a hero.

The choice between Bush versus Clinton became more complex when businessman Ross Perot jumped into the race. Perot was a billionaire who had broken into the national consciousness in a 1968 Fortune article entitled "Fastest, Richest Texan Ever." By the end of 1970, some fourteen national articles appeared screaming such claims as: "Ross Perot: Billionaire Patriot;" "What's Right with America;" "Ross Perot: Dallas Crusader;" and "Texas Breeds New Billionaire."[22] On February 20, 1992, Perot was the only guest on the *Larry King Live* show on CNN. According to King's account, the talk show host asked Perot whether he was thinking of running for the presidency and Perot said, "No." Then in the middle of the show, King asked if there were ever any circumstances under which Perot would run. Perot said if he could get on the ballot in all fifty states, then he would consider running for president.[23] It was another example of a cable television show breaking a major news story over the heads of the mainstream establishment.

The CNN switchboard lit up and the Perot candidacy was underway. Citizens all across the United States started Perot-for-president petitions and the national news media, ever alert for a dramatic turn of events, fueled the Perot phenomenon. The Texas billionaire appeared on the *Today* show and took questions from viewers. Host Katie Couric was bypassed as Perot set up a relationship with viewers and supporters. He was supposed to appear in the first hour, but his appearance was so successful the *Today* producers pushed Perot to continue on the show for a second hour.

Perot appeared on almost every other television show that he could find and took calls. Media watchers forgot that Clinton started the talk show circuit before Perot, appearing on *Donahue* and the *Today* show before Perot did. During Perot's phone-in questions on the *Today* show, not one question from viewers asked about Gennifer Flowers, marijuana, or the draft. Citizens did not ask any "horse-race" or strategic questions, but rather they focused on substantive issues.[24] Clinton fought back in the war of the talk shows, appearing on the *Arsenio Hall Show* playing saxophone with Hall's posse, and wearing dark shades. As Hall maintained, "If you break down the [demographics] and look at who watches my show, it sure beats standing on a caboose." Clinton appeared on MTV on June 16, 1992, to become the first presidential candidate in history to take questions from an audience of MTV viewers. It was here when an audience member asked Clinton the infamous question about whether he wore boxers or briefs.

Vice President Dan Quayle showed the integration of Hollywood and politics in 1992 when he argued that one of the reasons for the Los Angeles riots was the breakup of the family. Choosing a particularly poignant example about how Hollywood and the media perpetuated antifamily values, he cited what he considered the poor values of popular television character "Murphy Brown," a single woman who had a child out of wedlock.

For the next two days the media feeding frenzy became Dan Quayle versus "Murphy Brown." Comedians, journalists, activists, and columnists had a field day with Quayle. How dare he attack "Murphy Brown," who had better values than Quayle, according to some critics. Did the conservative vice president want "Murphy Brown" to have an abortion? Only in America could a politician get into so much trouble for attacking a fictional television character.[25]

That fall, "Murphy Brown" fired back. With a viewing audience of 70 million people, its highest ever, the episode incorporated Quayle's speech about family values and noted the importance of "commitment, caring, and love" in personal relationships. It was the ultimate merger of politics and entertainment. The episode culminated with the show's ending: dumping a truckload of potatoes at Quayle's home—a none-too-subtle jab at the vice president's spelling difficulties.[26] Quayle responded by sending the fictional "Murphy Brown" a baby present, which was opened on CBS "Morning News."

In looking at how America got to the point of an "infotainment culture," Carl Bernstein blamed the proliferation of talk shows and the rise of a celebrity pop culture he called "The Idiot Culture":

> For more than fifteen years we have been moving away from real journalism toward the creation of a sleazoid infotainment culture in which the lines between Oprah and Phil and Geraldo and Diane and even Ted, between the *New York Post* and *Newsday*, are too often indistinguishable. In this culture of journalistic titillation, we teach our readers and our viewers that the trivial is significant, that the lurid and loopy are more important than real news.[27]

In a similar vein, William Greider indicted the national news media and the passive audience of Americans who allowed this culture to exist. In his excellent analysis of the American political system, *Who Will Tell the People?*, Greider explains how the American system of lobbyists, PACs, sound bites, blow-dried politicians, sloppy media, and apolitical citizens does not work. He makes a clear statement about the problem of American MTV-like video politics in his section on "The Lost Generation."[28]

During his presidency, Bush often connected with American popular culture. He was a huge country and western music fan, and regularly fraternized with Randy Travis, Reba McEntire, Loretta Lynn, and the Oak Ridge Boys in the country music field. He shared campaign stops with them and some were invited to the White House.[29] Bush was a major sports fan who was photographed with sporting heroes and participated in all sorts of sports and activities during his presidency such as jogging, tennis, golf, and fishing. Bush was even reduced to the role of talk show guest, appearing on the TNN show, *Nashville Now*, hosted by Ralph Emery, sandwiched between entertainer Ricky Skaggs and other country and western entertainers.

In pop culture terms, Clinton had strong ties to the 1960s culture. He had done an Elvis Presley imitation on a New York radio station, and appeared on Arsenio Hall playing the saxophone. He answered questions for *Rolling Stone* and MTV. He liked all kinds of music including rock, country and western, soul, rhythm and blues, gospel, swing, and rap. He enjoyed taking his daughter Chelsea to see the latest movies.

Pop culture and celebrity politics intermingled with the fall election campaign. Bush appeared with movie actor Arnold Schwarzenegger, country star Ricky Skaggs, super hero Chuck Norris, and other conservative celebrities. Clinton went to Hollywood for a giant fund-raiser as all the liberals from California turned out to pay tribute to Clinton's lead in the polls. Barbra Streisand supported Clinton proudly. Election stories centered on the Dan Quayle–Murphy Brown battle. The *Murphy Brown* show won many Emmy Awards in 1992 and Quayle said the show owed him "big time" for all he had done. Dianne English, the creator of *Murphy Brown*, attacked Quayle during her Emmy acceptance. Candice Bergen, the star of *Murphy Brown*, thanked Vice President Quayle in a mocking way.

Celebrities began to appear on behalf of candidates everywhere during the final days of the campaign. Cher backed Perot and called to support him on *Larry King Live* twice. Bruce Willis appeared as a super hero for Bush on the president's final stops. Country and western singer Kathy Mattea appeared at a Clinton–Gore campaign rally in New Jersey just before election day. Local television listings in various newspapers showed where and when candidates could be found in the celebrity politics miniseries.

Throughout the campaign, the diversification of media outlets to talk radio, television, newspapers, newsweeklies, and Internet sites altered how candidates presented themselves to the public and the manner in which voters acquired political information. The hard news focus and mainstream media domination of the campaign receded before the onslaught of talk shows, celebrity campaigners, and a focus on background and character. It was a system that was high on entertainment value, but low on substance.

The 2000 presidential race between Al Gore and George W. Bush featured celebrities in abundance. Gore had the usual coterie of Hollywood stars at his side in the closing days of the campaign: Cher (back from her

Perot flirtation in 1992), Rob Reiner, Martin Sheen, Ben Affleck, and Whoopi Goldberg. Rock entertainer Jon Bon Jovi preceded the celebrity caravan by entertaining audiences until the vice president showed up. To one crowd, Bon Jovi announced why he was supporting Gore: "I wrote 'Living on a Prayer' during the Reagan era trickle-down economics. I don't want to go back," he explained.[30] Sheen appeared on the *Tonight Show* and showed videotapes of his arrest at a demonstration protesting Bush's planned Strategic Defense Initiative.[31] Gore himself answered questions from Queen Latifah regarding whether he preferred women in leather or lace. The answer, according to the vice president, was lace.[32]

Bush appeared on *Live with Regis* dressed like the host. The Texas governor relied on country western stars like Loretta Lynn and the Oak Ridge Boys, action movie entertainers such as Chuck Norris (who also had campaigned for Bush's father), and movie actors such as Bo Derek. As a clear example of a legacy politician, the third in line behind his father, President George Bush, and grandfather, Senator Prescott Bush, George W. Bush used his family's extensive fund-raising contacts to become the first major party nominee in several decades to forgo public financing of his general election.

When asked about a Bush dynasty, the Texas governor said, "Dynasty means something inherited. We inherited a good name, but you don't inherit a vote."[33] Yet these protestations aside, there is little doubt that Bush's financial advantages and name identification represented major boosts for his candidacy. These strengths propelled him out of the field of GOP contenders and insured that he was the one rated by reporters as the candidate to beat.

But perhaps the clearest example of celebrity politics came in the historic Senate race of Hillary Rodham Clinton. Seeking to become the only first lady in American history to win elective office in her own right, Clinton brought together a panoply of celebrities to assist her effort. At a New Year's Eve party attended by 350 people at the White House, the first lady was joined by Jack Nicholson and Muhammad Ali, among others.[34]

A fund-raiser for Mrs. Clinton featured former Buffalo Bills star defensive tackle, Bruce Smith. At a cost of $500, guests could meet Smith and mingle with Clinton supporters. Even though Smith had left the Bills and joined the Washington Redskins, one newspaper writer noted that "Clinton was hoping to strategically unveil the endorsement of Smith, a former stalwart with the Buffalo Bills. While she wasn't born in New York, at least she'll have a former New York player on her team."[35] The event demonstrated how clearly intertwined the worlds of celebrity sports and politics had become.

Another celebrity fund-raising auction for the first lady in New York attracted Yoko Ono, Christo, Jeff Koons, and Robert Rauschenberg.[36] Barbra Streisand organized a garden party fund-raiser for Mrs. Clinton that attracted scores of Hollywood bigwigs, including singer Diana Ross.[37] Another Hollywood fund-raiser headlined by Stevie Wonder, Whoopi

Goldberg, and Cher drew hundreds, including John Ritter, Angie Dickinson, Jon Voight, Dave Winfield, John Travolta, Carol Burnett, and Steve Allen. At the event, comedian Tom Arnold was asked what advice he would give the first lady. Showing the dangers of inviting humorists to political fundraisers, Arnold joked, "Don't pose nude."[38]

To conclude, it is clear that several aspects of the mass media have contributed to the emergence of the celebrity politics regime. The proliferation of media outlets, the emphasis on image-making and tabloid-style gossip, the ability of celebrities to sell newspapers, and the winnowing role performed by journalists give celebrities important advantages in the American political system. By bringing with them high name identification and the ability to curry favor with journalists, famous people have emerged as prominent candidates in a celebrity-saturated culture.

NOTES

1. Daniel Boorstin, *The Image: A Guide to Pseudo-Events in America* (New York: Atheneum Publishing, 1972), p. 57.
2. Orrin Klapp, *Heroes, Villains and Fools: The Changing American Character* (Englewood Cliffs, NJ: Prentice Hall, 1962), pp. 142–145.
3. Orrin Klapp, *Symbolic Leaders* (Chicago: Aldine Publishers, 1964), p. 252.
4. Bill Carter, "Final 'Survivor' May Star in Mean Quiz Show," *New York Times*, 11 January 2001, p. C-8.
5. Darrell M. West, *The Rise and Fall of the Media Establishment* (Boston: Bedford/St. Martin's Press, 2001).
6. Howard Kurtz, *Spin Cycle: Inside the Clinton Propaganda Machine* (New York: Free Press, 1998).
7. Holli A. Semetko, "The Role of Mass Media in Elections: What Can We Learn from 1988?" *The Political Science Teacher* (summer 1988), p. 18.
8. Robert Trott, "Chappaquiddick Tries to Forget 'Kennedy Bridge,'" *Toronto Star*, 15 July 1989, p. A-2.
9. Larry Sabato, Mark Stempel, and Robert Lichter, *Peep Show: Media and Politics in an Age of Scandal* (Lanhan, MD: Rowman & Littlefield, 2000) and Larry Sabato, *Feeding Frenzy: How Attack Journalism Has Transformed American Politics* (New York: Free Press, 1991).
10. Larry Sabato, Mark Stempel, and Robert Lichter, *Peep Show: Media and Politics in an Age of Scandal* (Lanhan, MD: Rowman & Littlefield, 2000).
11. David Broder, "Political Reporters in Presidential Politics," in *Presidential Politics*, ed. James Lengle and Byron Shafer (New York: St. Martin's, 1980).
12. Darrell M. West, *Patrick Kennedy: The Rise to Power* (Englewood Cliffs, NJ: Prentice Hall, 2000).
13. Alison Mitchell, "McCain Sure on Military Issues, Is Less Certain on Domestic Ones," *New York Times*, 9 February 2000, p. A-1.
14. David Weaver, Doris Graber, Maxwell McCombs, and Chaim Eyal, *Media Agenda-Setting in a Presidential Election* (New York: Praeger, 1981).

15. Edward Epstein, *News from Nowhere* (New York: Random House, 1973); Herbert Gans, *Deciding What's News* (New York: Pantheon, 1979); and Michael Robinson and Margaret Sheehan, *Over the Wire and on TV* (New York: Russell Sage Foundation, 1983).

16. Keith Blume, *The Presidential Election Show* (Massachusetts: Bergin and Garvey, 1985) and Neil Postman, *Amusing Ourselves to Death: Public Discourse in the Age of Show Business* (New York: Viking Penguin, 1985).

17. John Orman, "Yes, the Media Do Inform," in *Controversial Issues in Presidential Selection*, ed. Gary Rose (Albany, NY: The State University of New York Press, 1991), pp. 109–117.

18. Molly Ivins, *Shrub: The Short but Happy Political Life of George W. Bush* (New York: Vintage Books, 2000).

19. Robert Agranoff, *The New Style in Election Campaigns* (Boston: Holbrook Press, 1976); Kathleen Jamieson, *Packaging the Presidency* (New York: Oxford University Press, 1993); and Robert Spero, *The Duping of the American Voter: Dishonesty and Deception in Presidential Television Advertising* (New York: Lippincott, Crowell, 1980).

20. Judy Keen, "Conservative Struggles to Shake Off Image of Protest Candidate and Move beyond Bush," *USA Today*, 7 February 1992, p. 13-A.

21. See Richard Cohen, "Does the Beltway Defense of 'Beltway Buchanan' Constitute a Conflict of Interest?" *Bridgeport Post*, 8 February 1992, p. A-10 and see William Greider, "Buchanan Rethinks the American Empire," *Rolling Stone*, 6 February 1992, pp. 37–39.

22. See A. M. Louis, "Fastest, Richest Texan Ever," *Fortune*, November 1968, pp. 160–170; C. W. Wren, "Ross Perot: Billionaire Patriot," *Look*, 24 March 1976, pp. 28–32; Ross Perot, "What's Right with America," *Nation's Business*, July 1970, pp. 20–21; and "Ross Perot: Dallas Crusader," *Newsweek*, 13 April 1970, pp. 68–69.

23. Larry King, "How Perot's Quest Began," *USA Today*, 8 June 1992, p. 2-D.

24. Peter Johnson, "'Today' Happy to Have Candidates on the Line," *USA Today*, 10 June 1992, p. 3-D.

25. Andrew Rosenthal, "After the Riots: Quayle Says Riots Sprang from Lack of Family Values," *New York Times*, 20 May 1992, p. A-1.

26. Rick Dubrow, "'Murphy Brown' to Dan Quayle: Read Our Ratings," *Los Angeles Times*, 23 September 1992, p. F-1.

27. Carl Bernstein, "The Idiot Culture," *New Republic*, 8 June 1992, pp. 22–28.

28. William Greider, "The Lost Generation," in *Who Will Tell the People?* (New York: Simon & Schuster, 1992), pp. 307–330.

29. Michael Kelly, "Culture for the Presidential Candidate? It's Prescribed but Not in Lethal Doses," *International Herald Tribune*, 11 July 1992, p. 3.

30. *Providence Journal*, "Hollywood Sets Stage for Campaign Finale," 2 November 2000, p. A-2.

31. Caryn James, "Where Politics and Comedy Intermingle, the Punch Lines Can Draw Blood," *New York Times*, 4 November 2000, p. A-21.

32. Michiko Kakutani, "With the Guy Next Door in the Oval Office, the Presidency Shrinks Further," *New York Times*, 19 January 2001, p. A-17.

33. Roxanne Roberts, "Like Father, Like Sons," *Washington Post*, 16 December 2000, p. C-1.

34. Mary Jane Fine, "White House Guests to GOP," *New York Daily News*, 24 September 2000, p. 26.
35. Ed Henry, "Heard on the Hill," *Roll Call*, 29 June 2000.
36. George Rush and Joanna Molloy, "They're Canvassing for Hillary," *New York Daily News*, 10 May 2000, p. 18.
37. Joan Ryan, "Campaign 2000," *San Francisco Chronicle*, 15 August 2000, p. A-25.
38. Joel Siegel and Mitchell Fink, "First Lady Flexes Her Hollywood Star Appeal," *New York Daily News*, 13 August 2000, p. 8.

THE MONEY MACHINE

No element of celebrity politics is more crucial than the ability to raise money. With the high cost of political races and the amount of money required to broadcast ads and conduct polls, fund-raising is vital both for electoral and governing success. In the 2000 election, for example, candidates for federal office spent an unprecedented $2.5 billion, up $500 million from 1996. This included more than half a million each by the two national party committees and $300 million by outside groups such as the AFL-CIO, pharmaceutical companies, Planned Parenthood, and the Chamber of Commerce.

George W. Bush became the first candidate in U.S. history to raise $100 million from private donors. New Jersey candidate Jon Corzine spent $60.2 million of his own money to win a U.S. Senate seat, more than double the previous record of $27.5 million expended by Michael Huffington in a losing California Senate bid. A California House battle between Adam Schiff and James Rogan cost $10 million. Michael Bloomberg spent more than $76 million of his own money to become mayor of New York. The New York Senate race between Hillary Clinton and Rick Lazio ran up a joint tab of $68.6 million. Discussing that New York contest, long-time Democratic fund-raiser Harold Ickes admitted in regard to the unprecedented amount that "It even staggers me, and I'm pretty hard-core."[1]

The figures for government lobbying are no less striking. Companies, unions, and groups with a stake in influencing public policy devote around $2 billion a year to lobbying public officials, according to recent reports. Pharmaceutical companies, for example, spent over $70 million in 1999 alone lobbying Congress and the president. This was after the Clinton administration proposed an ambitious prescription drug bill that the industry feared.[2] If the measure were passed, drugmakers worried that it would drive down the price of medicines they produced and thereby wreak havoc on their sector.

Similar lobbying was undertaken by the tobacco industry. Big tobacco spends around $30 million each year to fight government actions it defines as detrimental to its business. This ranges from lobbying against legislation authorizing smoking bans in workplaces and restaurants to efforts seeking relief from antismoking lawsuits around the country.[3] With the unprecedented suits against tobacco companies over the past decade, the industry has gone both to Washington and state capitols seeking limits on its legal liability.[4] With its total liability reaching into the billions, the $30 million is a small price to pay for the beleaguered industry.

This spending undertaken by private interests is merely part of the "investment" theory of lobbying. While some give for ideological reasons, other groups invest resources in lobbying in hopes of gaining resources for their area. If troublesome regulations costing millions to a company are lifted or watered down, spending a few million dollars on lobbying is a cheap investment.[5] Or if legislation would impose new costs on a particular industry, lobbying to soften the blow would make good economic sense for the legions of companies affected.

With the need for large amounts of money to contest campaigns and policymaking, it is little wonder that celebrities have gained such clout in the political system. Simply by dint of their star appeal, celebrities are adept at raising money and attracting media attention to particular candidates and highlighting the importance of pressing causes. Putting a famous name on a fundraiser is a sure-fire way to sell tickets to the event. The combination of fame, glamour, and excitement is a time-tested recipe for successful money-raising, as evidenced by the fund-raising prowess of the new generation of Kennedys. Large numbers of political candidates and ideological causes employ celebrities to raise money, and celebrities themselves have jumped into running for office in part because of their well-demonstrated ability to raise money.

The power of money in American politics is not exactly novel. Fundraising clout always has been crucial to political success. In the eighteenth century, for example, George Washington and other politicians of that era raised cash in order to provide whiskey to supporters. It was a direct way to make sure that ordinary people sympathetic to a particular interest turned out at election time.

Throughout the nineteenth century, cash payoffs to legislators were routine during the policymaking process.[6] Railroad, oil, and manufacturing interests were famous for bribing government officials. If the issue were a right-of-way for a key rail line or a favorable tariff for a major industry, the most dependable and persuasive means of lobbying was the delivery of cold, hard cash.

The corruption of American politics eventually led muckraking journalists to write graphic exposes of the political bribery and extortion that was rampant in a number of cities and states. Writers such as Ida Tarbell and Lincoln Steffens described how business interests won benefits over common folk by manipulating the political system to their advantage. Although such journalists felt bribery and extortion were shameful, they found that such tactics were quite common up and down the American political system.

At the turn of the twentieth century, moneyman Mark Hanna employed a novel one-quarter percent quota on businesses by which they were expected to donate one-quarter of one percent of their operating capital to the Republican party in order to be eligible for government contracts. The money raised through these informal "taxes" helped enable the GOP to dominate the political system for several decades, virtually up until the Great Depression struck.

Senator Lyndon Johnson used money from the oil and gas industry to rise from being a dirt-poor Texan to becoming president of the United States. Along the way, he helped sympathetic industries and even won a sweetheart license for a new television station that served the state capital of Austin, Texas.[7]

Cash was crucial to the misdeeds that characterized Richard Nixon's Watergate abuses. Large amounts of secret contributions funded efforts to destabilize the candidacy of front-runner Ed Muskie and to spy on and collect negative information on other leading Democrats. Without access to large amounts of secret money, it is unlikely Nixon would have been able to engage in the "dirty tricks" that led up to the 1972 presidential election.[8]

But today, the combination of expensive campaigns, media domination of the political process, and the need to control the message has accentuated the importance of money and raised the political status of those such as celebrities who are in a position to raise vast sums of money. Celebrities have gone from being people who were famous in nonpolitical fields to individuals who use their fame to raise money and advance political causes.

Changes in news management strategies highlight the need to raise large amounts of money in the contemporary period. It used to be that candidates relied on public relations strategies geared to placing favorable stories about themselves in the press. An army of PR consultants and media advisors specialized in working with political figures to generate good press for those people. Through positive works, charitable contributions, and new policy ideas, politicians sought to create sympathetic articles about themselves that would enhance their political careers and make it possible for them to run for public office.

For conventional politicians without the advantages of celebrityhood, this generally took years. Politicians were required to work their way up slowly over a long period of time. Under the rules of career development that marked most of the nineteenth and early-twentieth centuries, unknown politicians started their careers by running for local office, and then as they became better known, moved up to prominent state and federal positions. It could take fifteen to twenty years to be in a position where the individual could run for a major office, such as governor, U.S. Senator, or U.S. House member.

It particularly was important that there be no scandals or negative coverage that would tarnish the figure's personal image. If the public official developed a reputation for shadiness or opportunistic political dealings, it became difficult for that person to move from local to national politics. Or if the candidate was seen as lacking the proper temperament, it would be nearly impossible to advance politically.

Today, in contrast, celebrities have proven that it is possible to circumvent the normal pattern of news management and career advancement.[9] If an individual starts by being well-known, wealthy, and having access to financial support from other backers, that person can run for governor or senator without the usual political apprenticeship of working his or her way up through lower-level offices.

A number of celebrities such as John Glenn, Jim Bunning, Jesse Jackson, Jr., and Steve Largent began their political careers by running for the Senate or House. Due to their high name identification and fund-raising capabilities, they were able to leapfrog the usual career patterns and win a national office in their initial try for elective office.

For example, John Glenn went from being an astronaut to running successfully for the U.S. Senate. First elected in 1974, Glenn combined a down-to-earth appeal with star power arising from his record as one of the first Americans in space. Citizens flocked to his campaign events and voted for him in large numbers. He ran for president in 1984, but lost the Democratic nomination to Walter Mondale. Glenn was not seriously challenged in the Senate until he retired from public life.

What Glenn and other famed nonpoliticos have demonstrated is that money allows candidates to bypass traditional public relations strategies and put themselves in a position where they can control their own message. As journalists have moved toward more gossipy and scandal-oriented coverage, politicians no longer automatically can count on favorable treatment from the press. Even celebrities experience both the upside and downside of fame in dealing with the media.[10] Just as famous people make good copy when they perform positive deeds, they also can sell newspapers through personal problems, scandals, and misdeeds.

No family better than the Kennedys has demonstrated the ability to be the beneficiaries as well as the victims of the press at various points in time. Journalists ceaselessly have puffed up the Kennedys by covering them as entertainment figures and playing up the myth of Camelot. Yet during Chappaquiddick, William Kennedy Smith's sexual assault trial, and Michael Kennedy's affair with the family's baby-sitter, the press sensationalized Kennedy travails and blamed the entire family for the sins of the few.

With around-the-clock news cycles and 24-hour news stations, politicians of all stripes have learned that it is important to control not just the content but the timing of political appeals. Even with sympathetic reporters, it is virtually impossible to guarantee that a favorable story will appear when it is needed or in the form the candidate would prefer. The vagaries of the news cycle plus the tendency of reporters to cover events from a scandal framework make it risky for candidates or political leaders to assume press coverage will be favorable and timely. For those reasons, candidates raise large sums of money so they can control message delivery and their public images, both of which are crucial for political success.[11]

In a variety of ways, celebrities and legacies have advantages in terms of general image formation and fund-raising. By dint of their fame, they bring a reputation to the public sphere. They are well-known, have prominent associations in the public mind, and are adept at building a positive political profile. Typically, they either are rich or have access to wealthy people willing to support their cause. It is easier to attract press coverage and convince fans to attend their fund-raisers. Donors love to associate with entertainers they have seen on television or in movies, or sports stars who have high visibility.

The best examples of this kind of advantage can be found in the case of legacy candidates. Individuals such as Jesse Jackson, Jr., Harold Ford, Jr., Patrick Kennedy, and Hillary Clinton have found it much easier to raise money and gain access to political circles because of their last names. Being part of a famous political family put them within the right networks and made it possible for them to piggyback on the electoral success of their forebears.

When Jesse Jackson, Jr., first ran for Congress in a 1995 special election, he benefited from having a famous last name and being able to raise money from supporters of his father. Prominent personalities such as Johnnie Cochran, Aretha Franklin, and Bill Cosby contributed to his campaign. Jesse Jackson, Sr., made some of his old advisors such as Frank Watkins available to his son. Using the slogan "Let a New Generation Arise," the younger Jackson ran against one of his area's most experienced politicians and won. On his first day as a congressman, he was asked if he would have been victorious if his name were Jesse Jones. Appreciating the irony of the question, Jackson replied by joking, "Ask Patrick Kennedy."[12]

It was a question that Patrick Kennedy had been forced to answer during his initial congressional contest in 1994. Like Jackson, Kennedy mined his father's Rolodex in many ways: getting an early endorsement from Dick Gephardt, holding Washington, D.C., fund-raisers with prominent labor officials such as John Sweeney of the AFL-CIO, and receiving advice from big-name politicos. While the Kennedy name cuts many ways (the family is loved by many and hated by others), the Kennedys have positive associations in the eyes of many Americans, especially those living in the Northeast. For those individuals, the family name is synonymous with public service and concern for the downtrodden. Kennedy was able to draw on this support and raise over $1 million for his first congressional race.

In an era where politics is expensive and cash is king, celebrities bring distinctive advantages to the task of political fund-raising. They have high voter recognition, favorable public images, access to financial resources, and the ability to attract positive press coverage. Both legacies and famous non-politicos have experience dealing with celebrityhood and often are comfortable standing in the public spotlight.[13]

Since they operate in a popular culture that glorifies fame and with a media geared toward the rich and famous, celebrities are perfectly positioned to take advantage of the contemporary political situation. They play to an audience that is susceptible to celebrity appeals and a media that loves to cover the ups and downs of prominent people. Just as a series of military generals were politically successful at winning national office in the eighteenth and nineteenth centuries, Hollywood and sporting stars today are adept at raising money and cultivating public attention. It is hard to match their star power in a culture obsessed with celebrityhood.

Not only do celebrity entertainers have strengths when they themselves run for office, but also celebrity entertainers have proved to be enormously helpful at contributing money to conventional politicians. Indeed, as the costs of campaigning have risen and politicians have been forced to raise money to communicate their messages to the general public, celebrities have become crucial to the act of raising money. Without their prominent names, it is not at all clear whether certain politicians would have gone as far as they did.

Since 1972, when Warren Beatty organized a group of stars to work for George McGovern, celebrities have emerged as permanent fixtures on the campaign trail. Beatty and Ode record executive Lou Adler began the first of a series of celebrity fundraisers for McGovern that year. The "new Hollywood" celebrities like Jack Nicholson, Rob Reiner, and Goldie Hawn were the ushers at the shows. The entertainment was provided by James Taylor, Carole King, Quincy Jones, and Barbra Streisand. In a performance at Madison Square Garden in New York, the McGovern concerts raised $250,000 with acts like the reunions of Simon and Garfunkel as well as Peter, Paul and Mary. Richard Nixon countered with performances at the 1972 Republican National Convention by Sammy Davis, Jr., and the Osmond Brothers.

The 1976 celebrity scorecard showed rock stars going for Democrats and old Hollywood stars supporting Ronald Reagan's challenge of incumbent Gerry Ford. Ford had support from Sonny Bono. Reagan had much of conservative Hollywood behind his candidacy. Progressive Democrats like Morris Udall had Mary Travers and Harry Belafonte as supporters, while candidate Fred Harris had Arlo Guthrie and Harry Chapin.

But the real celebrity contest was between front-runner Jimmy Carter and California Governor Jerry Brown. Carter had support from Phil Walden and Capricorn records, and rock acts like the Allman Brothers Band and the

Marshall Tucker Band who endorsed the former governor of Georgia. Hunter S. Thompson supported Carter and later at Carter's inaugural ball, Cher, Greg Allman, and even John Lennon were invited as celebrities tied into Carter.

Among the celebrities contributing money to Carter's campaign were James Brown ($500 contribution); Johnny Cash ($1,000); June Carter Cash ($1,000); Michael Douglas ($1,000); Charlie Daniels ($250); Mark Goodman ($1,000); rock promoter Bill Graham ($1,000), and Burt Lancaster ($1,000).

Jerry Brown had rock concert money from his friends Linda Ronstadt, Jackson Browne, and the Eagles. Chicago and Helen Reddy also sent some rock money his way. Among Brown's celebrity contributors were Herb Alpert ($1,000), Warren Beatty ($1,000), Al Jardine of the Beach Boys ($500), Steve Lawrence ($500), Burgess Meredith ($250), Carroll O'Connor ($1,600), Sam Peckinpah ($250), Helen Reddy ($1,000), and Sugar Ray Robinson ($150).

Carter won the 1976 celebrity sweepstakes and tried to keep close contact with his celebrity backers for the 1980 campaign. By 1980, Carter had a whole new list of celebrity supporters because he was the incumbent president seeking reelection. Carter was challenged again by Jerry Brown, but Brown's list of celebrities was much shorter that year. Befitting the limited nature of his political support, Brown's most prominent celebrities included rock star Linda Ronstadt, the Eagles, and activist Jane Fonda. This was a far shorter list than had been the case in his 1976 presidential campaign.

The major celebrity challenge came from supporters of Ted Kennedy, who hoped for a return to the Camelot days. This included individuals such as Lauren Bacall, Henry Fonda, Angie Dickinson, Al Hirt, Rafer Johnson, Carroll O'Connor, Goldie Hawn, and Jack Lemmon. Carter turned back Kennedy's challenge by using his celebrity supporters, which included Willie Nelson, Johnny Cash, Muhammad Ali, Shana Alexander, Stephen Stills, Ansel Adams, Tammy Wynette, and Mary Tyler Moore.

On the Republican side, George Bush, running in 1980, had support from Tammy Grimes, Lionel Hampton, Nolan Ryan, Tom Seaver, Digger Phelps, Bud Wilkinson, and Jim Otis. Republican challenger John Anderson from Illinois was going nowhere as a member of the Republican also-rans, but then he announced he was running as a third-party, independent candidate. He received celebrity media boosts from *Saturday Night Live*, the *New York Times*, and Doonesbury. Quickly, celebrities like Tom Petty and the Heartbreakers, Norman Lear, Cliff Robertson, Paul Newman, Joanne Woodward, Grant Tinker, and Kurt Vonnegut, Jr., jumped on the Anderson bandwagon.

However, no Republican, Democrat, or even an Independent could compete with the celebrity field of supporters for actor Ronald Reagan. Among Reagan backers for the successful 1980 campaign were Morey Amsterdam, Ray Bolger, James Cagney, Hoagy Carmichael, Robert Conrad, Zsa Zsa Gabor, Rocky Graziano, Merle Haggard, Art Linkletter, Tony Martin, Ginger Rogers, Gloria Swanson, Loretta Young, and Efrem Zimbalist, Jr. One very strange Reagan backer was Neil Young who thought Carter was a wimp and that Reagan was better macho material.

In 1984, the celebrity race showed black American stars rallying around Rev. Jesse Jackson while Gary Hart received support from younger, former Kennedy-wing celebrities and Mondale got the older Democratic party celebrity support. Reagan and Bush called upon the same celebrity backers that they had garnered for the 1980 election and received the same victorious fund-raising results.

With the wide-open 1988 presidential election race, a new pattern of celebrity participation developed. On the Republican side, candidate Al Haig could call on celebrity support from John Gavin, Billy Dee Williams, and Mort Sahl. Jack Kemp had backing from Robert Conrad, Mike Connors, and Mickey Rooney. Robert Dole had support from Joan Collins, Lynda Carter, Clint Eastwood, Charlton Heston, Tom Selleck, and Michael Landon. Reverend Pat Robertson had backing from country-western figures Ricky Skaggs, Pat Boone, Roy Rogers, and Dale Evans. George Bush was supported for the Republican nomination by Lionel Hampton, Cheryl Ladd, and Frank Sinatra with the understanding that if he would get the Republican nomination then all the celebrities that supported Reagan-Bush in 1980 and 1984 would also support Bush in 1988 after the convention.

On the Democratic side, Gary Hart had early support from Jack Nicholson, Warren Beatty, Goldie Hawn, and John Forsythe, but his campaign folded in the days after he and Donna Rice became headline scandal figures. Paul Simon, U.S. senator from Illinois, had support from Carly Simon, Whoopi Goldberg, Margot Kidder, Christopher Reeve, and Hugh Hefner before it became clear that he did not have a chance to win. Bruce Babbitt from Arizona had celebrity backing from actors Robert Redford, Ted Danson, and Pearl Bailey. Massachusetts governor Michael Dukakis was backed by Olympia Dukakis, Sally Field, Richard Gere, Art Garfunkel, and Leonard Nimoy before he received the Democratic nomination. Jesse Jackson received support from celebrities like Bill Cosby, Aretha Franklin, Roberta Flack, Kris Kristofferson, Casey Kasem, and Elizabeth Montgomery.

During the Clinton years, Democrats made a point of cultivating Hollywood money givers. Among the stars who spent time at the White House and supported party efforts were Barbra Streisand, Ted Danson, Carly Simon, James Taylor, Steven Spielberg, Michael Douglas, Whoopi Goldberg, and David Geffen. Indeed, Clinton made a priority out of spending a lot of time in Hollywood and shielding the industry from attacks regarding excessive sex and violence in the entertainment industry. As conservatives complained about declining values in American public life and a loss of morality, Clinton pushed for industry self-regulation and a television rating system, as opposed to formal government regulation.[14] He argued that technological innovations such as the "V-chip" would be helpful by allowing parents to program their television sets to screen out objectionable material.

In return, Hollywood responded with enthusiastic support for the former Arkansas governor. Not only did individual stars give hard-money gifts to Democratic candidates, but also they became some of the largest soft-money supporters of the Democratic party. Spielberg, for example, donated hundreds of thousands of dollars in unrestricted contributions to the Democratic party. His production company, DreamWorks SKG, gave $1 million to Democratic candidates around the country in 2000.[15]

The same was true for Jane Fonda. She made history in the 2000 election cycle by donating $12 million to abortion rights organizations so they could run issue ads in selected congressional races. It was one of the largest contributions from an individual in recent memory for someone who was not financing his or her own election effort. That year, it was dwarfed only by the $20 million that computer magnate Tim Draper devoted to a California initiative campaign promoting school vouchers.[16]

In looking at the overall pattern of campaign contributions over the past decade, entertainers associated with television, movies, and music gave Democrats $10 million in 1992, compared to $3 million that went to Republicans. In 1996, Democrats received $11 million, compared to $7 million for the GOP. In 2000, Hollywood delivered $20 million to Democrats and $13 million to Republicans.[17]

Over the past decade, the television, movie, and music industries raised around $95 million for electioneering, with 65 percent going to Democrats and 35 percent to Republicans. Forty-three million came from individuals, $16 million from political action committees, and $36 million was in the form of soft-money contributions to the parties. From the modest amount of $5 million in 1990 came contributions of $13 million in 1992, $9 million in 1994, $18 million in 1996, $16 million in 1996, and $33 million in the 2000 elections.[18] The last figure represented nearly a three-fold increase in giving from the entertainment industry.

These gifts were important as more and more citizens grew concerned over the amount of gratuitous sex and violence that appeared on television and in movies and music. Campaign contributions were a way to guarantee access when Washington politicians attacked Hollywood for what was viewed as declining moral standards in American society. Gifts did not guarantee the politician would vote the Hollywood position of libertarianism when it came to entertainment content, but large donors typically got their calls returned and their requests for meetings answered affirmatively.

In 2000, Hollywood delivered $1 million in hard-money contributions to Gore's campaign and nearly $800,000 to Bush. Top givers in 2000 included Joseph Seagram & Sons ($2 million; 66 percent of which went to Democrats), Time Warner ($1.8 million; 73 percent of which went to Democrats), Walt Disney ($1.4 million; of which 59 percent went to Democrats), Saban Entertainment ($1.3 million; all of which was given to Democrats), and the DreamWorks team of Steven Spielberg, Jeffrey Katzenberg, and David Geffen ($1 million; all of which was donated to Democrats).[19]

Gore's celebrity donors included seventeen Academy Award winners (such as Kevin Costner, Tom Hanks, Jack Nicholson, and Warren Beatty), two members of the *Dallas* show (Larry Hagman and Donna Mills), and the entire Frank Zappa family. Bush's high-profile donors included country music performers Loretta Lynn, Larry Gatlin, and Joe Bonsall of the Oak Ridge Boys as well as CBS sports broadcaster Jim Nantz. Green party candidate Ralph Nader attracted gifts from Susan Sarandon, Paul Newman, and Warren Beatty.[20]

In general, entertainment figures are more sympathetic to the Democratic party because it typically has taken more of a "hands-off" position on policy issues related to content restrictions and is more liberal on lifestyle issues such as gay rights. Republican worries about declining values and low morality sometimes have resulted in policy proposals seen as unfavorable to Hollywood movie, television, and music interests.

However, Senator Joe Lieberman, Gore's nominee for vice president in the Democratic party, attracted attention with his frequent comments that V-chips and voluntary rating systems were insufficient to protect fundamental American values. Joining forces with conservative writer William Bennett, Lieberman asked major record manufacturers to stop making and distributing rap and heavy metal videos with such inflammatory language.

It was a movement that created great cause for concern within Hollywood about possible censorship of entertainment products. One of the reasons why entertainment celebrities donated so much money to the Democratic party was the belief that Democrats would help protect the industry against conservative calls for censorship.[21] After Lieberman joined the Democratic ticket as vice president, however, he downplayed his earlier criticism of Hollywood and moved more in line with libertarian sentiments within his party. The shift was a vivid demonstration of how important Hollywood money had become to the major parties.

NOTES

1. *Minneapolis Star Tribune*, "First Post-Election Finance Totals Boggle the Mind, Break Records Left and Right," 8 December 2000, p. 22-A.
2. Paul Heldman, "Drugmakers Spend Big to Lobby Lawmakers," *Chicago Sun-Times*, 23 July 2000, p. 46.
3. Darrell M. West, *Checkbook Democracy: How Money Corrupts Political Campaigns* (Boston: Northeastern University Press, 2000), pp. 134–135.
4. Barry Meier and Emily Yellin, "Big Tobacco Is Lobbying the States for Help," *New York Times*, 20 March 2000, p. A-20.
5. Darrell M. West and Burdett Loomis, *The Sound of Money* (New York: Norton, 1998).
6. Michael Johnston, *Political Corruption and Public Policy in America* (Monterey, CA: Brooks/Cole Publishing Company, 1982).
7. Robert Caro, *Lyndon Johnson: The Rise to Power* (New York: Knopf, 1982).
8. Darrell M. West, *Checkbook Democracy: How Money Corrupts Political Campaigns* (Boston: Northeastern University Press, 2000), pp. 62–63.

9. David Canon, *Actors, Athletes, and Astronauts* (Chicago: University of Chicago Press, 1990).

10. Darrell M. West, *Patrick Kennedy: The Rise to Power* (Englewood Cliffs, NJ: Prentice Hall, 2000).

11. Darrell M. West, *Checkbook Democracy: How Money Corrupts Political Campaigns* (Boston: Northeastern University Press, 2000).

12. Laura Blumenfeld, "The Son Also Rises: Jesse Jackson, Jr., Isn't Following in Anybody's Footsteps. He Knows the Way," *Washington Post*, 3 January 1996, p. B-1.

13. David Marshall, *Celebrity and Power: Fame in Contemporary Culture* (Minneapolis: University of Minnesota Press, 1997).

14. William J. Bennett, *The Book of Virtues: A Treasury of Great Moral Stories* (New York: Simon & Schuster, 1993).

15. Center for Responsive Politics Web site, www.opensecrets.org, January 24, 2001, industry breakdowns.

16. Ruth Marcus, "Election Spending," *Bergen County Record*, 6 November 2000, p. A-10.

17. Center for Responsive Politics Web site, www.opensecrets.org, January 2, 2001, industry breakdowns.

18. Center for Responsive Politics Web site, www.opensecrets.org, January 2, 2001, industry breakdowns.

19. Center for Responsive Politics Web site, www.opensecrets.org, January 2, 2001, industry breakdowns.

20. Center for Responsive Politics, "That's Entertainment: A Look at Celebrity Donors to the Presidential Candidates," www.opensecrets.org, January 22, 2001.

21. Art Berman, "Arts and Entertainment Reports," *Los Angeles Times*, 30 May 1996, p. F-2 and Richard Harrington, "Guilty: Free Speech in the First Degree," *Washington Post*, 9 June 1996, p. G-4.

THE CELEBRITY PRESIDENCY

One key aspect of celebrity politics in the post–World War II period has been the emergence of television and the enormous ramifications of the electronic medium for the office of the presidency. From the time that it first appeared on the national scene, television has had major consequences for how our political system functions and for the ability of celebrity politicians to achieve political success. The so called "magic lantern" altered the types of qualities Americans looked for in its leaders and the types of individuals they chose to be president. Candidates with famous last names clearly benefited from these changes, as witnessed by the election of several recent presidents.

Prior to 1960, when television started to emerge as a major communications avenue for national leaders, more people got their public affairs information from newspapers. In 1959, for example, more people indicated they received most of their information from newspapers and found them to be more believable than television. Within ten years, though, these numbers had reversed. More people tuned into television and found it to be a believable news source compared to newspapers.[1]

At the same time, newspaper subscription levels started to drop. From their historical high point of 37 percent of the population subscribing to a daily newspaper in 1947, subscriptions have sunk to 22 percent currently. Conversely, the numbers of people owning television sets shot up. In 1950, only 9 percent of American households had a television. By 1960, this figure had jumped to 88 percent.[2]

The rise of television radically altered citizen perceptions about leadership and definitions of celebrity status. If one did not appear on television, it was difficult to be celebrated in our society. Events that were not covered on television might just as well not have occurred. Citizens relied on television to portray American reality as newspaper readership fell.[3] Starting around 1960 and continuing to this day, television emerged as the major definer of public reality.

In this situation, it is no surprise that television transformed the types of individuals who held the office of the presidency.[4] As early as 1952, the stage was set for the period of celebrity presidents. Dwight Eisenhower emerged as the celebrity World War II hero who would dare to be president. In so doing, he followed the lead of famous nineteenth-century generals such as Andrew Jackson and Ulysses Grant who became president. In each of these cases, the personality of the candidate became more important than ideological concerns, but especially so in the television era. Eisenhower ushered in "affective" candidate-oriented politics in which candidates campaigned based on personal likeability. Democrats in large numbers crossed over to vote for the "I like Ike" ticket. The result was that Eisenhower won in a landslide and became the first president systematically to exploit the then new medium of television.

Eisenhower's vice presidential candidate, Richard Nixon, introduced what became a standard genre of public life in the television era, the *mea culpa* address. In 1952, the *New York Post* reported that California businessmen had raised an $18,000 slush fund for him. Nixon initially replied that his critics were communists who were out to smear him. When the controversy failed to go away and Eisenhower pushed him to go public with a defense, Nixon turned to television for a tearful explanation about what had happened. Nixon delivered his famous "Checker's speech," a staged non-apology confession that worked to save Nixon's career.

This became the televised model of direct communication between politician to citizen to explain a personal problem. With his wife seated next to him, Nixon explained that the slush fund "was wrong, just not illegal." He pointed out that none of the money had gone for his personal use and that no one had garnered special favors in return for the gifts. In what became the emotional high point in his defense, Nixon noted that the one personal gift he had accepted was a small cocker spaniel sent from Texas that his six-year-old daughter Tricia adored. Defiantly, he refused to send that present back because "the kids, like all kids, love the dog and I just want to say this right now, that regardless of what they say about it, we're gonna keep it." The outpouring of public support following the address was so strong that Eisenhower kept him on the GOP ticket and Nixon was elected vice president.[5]

With television proliferating throughout American society, John F. Kennedy took the star system in celebrity politics to new heights. After his impressive performance in televised debates with Richard Nixon, Kennedy gained the White House. His delivery during the televised debates helped him win the undecided, independent vote because of his image of being a cool, calm, tanned matinee idol. In contrast to a pasty-looking Nixon, Kennedy came across as more youthful and vigorous, and as a leader capable of getting the country moving again after the staid period of the Eisenhower years.

Once in the White House, Kennedy presided over an air of glamour and excitement, while Jackie Kennedy provided the model for the elegant, fashionable, lovely First Lady. In part through connections of his brother-in-law, actor Peter Lawford, Kennedy brought many Hollywood stars to the White House. Movie star Marilyn Monroe attracted much attention when she sang "Happy Birthday, Mr. President" to Kennedy while the cameras rolled. That and other similar scenes helped Kennedy perpetuate the image of a president with star qualities. Kennedy went to great lengths to make sure reporters covered his administration with an image of fashion and political chic.

It would be years later when Americans found out about JFK's extramarital affairs with Judith Campbell, Marilyn Monroe, and others. Reporters were aware of the president's dalliances, but did not treat the behavior as newsworthy. Instead, the actions were treated as private and not to be disclosed to the general public.[6]

Since that time, celebrity presidencies emerged full-blown, both in positive and negative directions. Television made celebrities of many different presidents from Reagan to Clinton and George W. Bush. American politics became framed as a series of entertainment soap operas, complete with drama, comedy, and sometimes tragedy, a tendency that writer Neil Postman documented in his book, *Amusing Ourselves to Death: Public Discourse in the Age of Show Business*.[7] With its news, current events, and political programs, reporters cover presidents and other national leaders as an entertainment art form. According to Norman Corwin, television shows and the entertainment values of news have contributed greatly to the process of "trivializing America." In his view, television has helped the process in the United States where the end result has been the "triumph of mediocrity."[8] As former NBC newsman and former presidential press secretary to Gerald Ford, Ron Nesson has observed that television news is dominated by "too much trivia, too little substance."[9]

Television is a medium that brings us regular updates on *Entertainment Tonight, USA Today, People, US, Hard Copy, A Current Affair, Inside Edition*, the network news, and CNN about what entertainment celebrities are doing for a political cause or for politicians, and updates on personal information about politicians to keep their celebrity alive. This dramatic change in reporting about American popular culture because of its sheer magnitude and intensity has helped create new political heroes who are celebrities and new celebrities who are marketed as politicos. Sometimes, journalists also have participated in the downfall of celebrity politicians.

The impact of our televised celebrity political system made it possible for a former actor (Ronald Reagan) to become president of the United States, with help by a coterie of public relations specialists.[10] Reagan already had a celebrity image before he came to the White House in 1981. He had been a supporting actor and sometimes leading man in the Hollywood films of the 1940s and early 1950s. In the 1950s, he became a pitchman for General Electric. He broadcast baseball games in the 1930s on radio, and used his movie-star looks to become a celebrity banquet speaker. In the 1960s he became the governor of California, and in the 1970s he remained in the public eye as a speaker, columnist, politician, presidential candidate, and conservative celebrity. By the time he ran against Jimmy Carter in 1980, he had the benefit of some forty years of being in the public eye.

As president, Reagan combined a masterful use of television and radio with a great sense of pseudo-event theatrics. Indeed, he threw himself into the role of president as much as he worked himself up for the role of George Gipp in the *Knute Rockne* movie. Reagan became an outstanding performer in the drama of national political life. The photo opportunities and the dramatic backdrops like the Statue of Liberty or the demilitarized zone between North Korea and South Korea became Hollywood sets for Reagan. He even made it a standard practice to use successful movie sound bites in his own addresses such as throwing down a challenge to Congress by saying in his best Clint Eastwood fashion, "Go ahead and make my day." He asked support for citizens at the University of Notre Dame during a speech "to win one for the Gipper."

It was said by reporters in Washington that Reagan, along with his wife, Nancy, had restored glamour to the White House. They were the most beautiful storybook couple to live in the White House since the Kennedys. The Reagans invited celebrity friends to dinner and included many stars from the entertainment industry. In 1983 Reagan starred in an NBC television celebration for Bob Hope's eightieth birthday. He made small talk and told some funny jokes and stories about the comedian.[11] Nancy Reagan even emerged as a celebrity in her own right, appearing on an episode of "Diff'rent Strokes" and leading the "Just Say No" anti-drug campaign.

In the popular press covered by stories from the *Reader's Guide to Periodical Literature*, there were more articles about Ronald Reagan than appeared about any other American president in the twentieth century up to that time. For example, in the specific area of congressional relations stories about the American president that were published in the periodical press from 1968 to 1982, Richard Nixon averaged 19.6 stories per year, Jimmy Carter averaged 34.9 stories per year and Ronald Reagan averaged 134 stories per year.[12]

Obviously, writers covering the presidency found Reagan to be the best celebrity copy available. These reporters helped make the Reagan legend even bigger than it already was. He was the "winner" against Carter, Grenada, Libya, and the Sandinistas, and he was a "survivor" who confounded political enemies, assassins, and Democrats. The president was popular, well-liked, amiable, witty, and well-known.

Reagan's celebrity status and his personal popularity made it virtually impossible for the media to hold the president accountable for his behavior. From the very beginning of his administration, the Reagan team tried to keep information and secrets from the American people at the same time they tried to project and publicize the Reagan image as the "Great Communicator." For example, during the invasion of Grenada in 1983, the Reagan administration kept the American press out so as to keep people in doubt about the nature of the attack.[13] Compared with other recent presidents with respect to secrecy, the Reagan administration ranked with Richard Nixon for showing the most compulsive behavior toward secrecy. Yet little of this was publicized by the mainstream press during Reagan's presidency, and he often was glorified in highly personalistic terms.

Reagan made verbal mistakes and uttered statements that were totally inaccurate. For this behavior, which might have doomed more mortal politicians, he was treated by the press not as a liar but as a "Great Communicator."[14] Reporters picked up the label for him of "the teflon president" in 1983 when Pat Schroeder, U.S. representative, labeled him as such in her criticisms of the media's inability to make Reagan account for his actions. At the time, some journalists feared Reagan was "sinking into senility," but did not report it publicly.[15]

The former California governor maximized the strategy of speaking directly to the American people on radio and television to minimize the media's filtering ability and editing processes shown in newscasts. To complement this strategy, Reagan often hid from the press more than any other president in the modern era or pretended he could not hear shouted questions over the whirling blades of his waiting helicopter. He held the fewest press conferences per year of any recent chief executive up to that point. Reagan had 6.5 press conferences per year, while Nixon had 6.6 per year. These numbers were significantly lower than John Kennedy's 22.6, Lyndon Johnson's 26.1, Gerald Ford's 16.1 and Jimmy Carter's 14.7 press conferences per year.[16]

Reagan's handlers tried to limit his off-the-cuff exchanges with reporters during photo opportunities and reporters were kept behind ropes when the president's helicopter landed, not for security reasons, but because he might have to answer questions posed by White House correspondents. During the Reagan years, Larry Speakes, the president's press secretary became the *voice* of the Reagan administration more so than any other press secretary. In 1985, after one of Reagan's impromptu remarks about the Palestinian Liberation Organization, Speakes quickly issued a press clarification stating an extraordinary reality when he told reporters, "Ladies and Gentlemen, the President's statements do not reflect the policy of the Reagan administration."[17]

The Reagan administration tried to manipulate political symbols to help in the public relations efforts. Reagan used the Statue of Liberty, the 1984 Olympics, a *Rambo* movie, and even Bruce Springsteen for his own partisan political purposes to exploit patriotism. In 1984 he held a ceremony to celebrate the one-year anniversary of the victory in Grenada, but there was no mention of the marines who had died during the Beirut Massacre in 1983. Reagan even engaged in the first ever live, prime-time bombing during the national news cycles in April 1986. The national news anchors did not even realize how the Reagan team had manipulated the timing of the bombing to coincide with the national news.[18]

In part because of his previous experience in the entertainment industry, Reagan showed an uncanny ability to manipulate the public space on television and avoid political scrutiny. He was not made to account for selling arms to Iran in order to free American hostages. He was not made to account for the resupply operation for the Contras in Nicaragua in violation of the Boland Amendment of 1984. He did not have to account for unbalanced budget requests or savings and loans failures. He did not have to account for Housing and Urban Development scandals, and he did not have to account for lack of dealing with problems of environment, drugs, crime, racism, education, AIDS, homelessness, health care, unemployment, and the widening gap between rich and poor in this country. He became the quintessential media president who elevated style and image over substance with the help of an uncritical, protective American establishment media.

If Reagan dominated the 1980s, it was Jesse Jackson who provided the video alternative to Reaganism in the 1980s. Jackson had been a political celebrity from the 1960s civil rights movement and the 1970s black struggle. Jackson's charismatic personality appeared in news accounts and on talk shows of the 1970s. In the 1980s he reached new heights of political celebrity by his two campaigns for the American presidency.

Jackson's 1984 campaign brought militant, social-movement politics to a new level within American presidential politics. Rather than pressuring Republicans and Democrats to respond to the demands of social-movement politics, out-groups in American life could rally around Jesse Jackson's "Rainbow Coalition." Jackson tried to unite blacks, feminists, workers, old people, Native Americans, Hispanics, Asian immigrants, and Arab Americans, among other groups.

On the issues, Jackson was the most progressive major presidential candidate to run since socialist Norman Thomas. Had Jackson been a white candidate, his progressive issue stands would have been demeaned by presidential watchers in a conservative country, in much the same fashion as George McGovern was portrayed as a radical in the 1972 election. Instead, Jackson was portrayed in the major media as the *black* candidate for president.

In fact, the major media concentrated so much on Jackson's "blackness" that it de-emphasized his liberalism and also missed a major story on his candidacy that would have centered around church and state issues. If Jackson had been covered in more conventional ways, major presidential watchers would have questioned his ability to keep church issues separate from state matters as a preacher and potential president. However, this issue was not even raised since Jackson was covered as a black civil rights activist who decided to run for president.

Jackson's campaign featured a charismatic orator and short, ten-second sound bites that were perfect for national television coverage. The Jackson organization pulled off some unbelievable media coups like his European tour of September 1983; negotiations with Syria to release Lieutenant Robert Goodman in January 1984; his strong showing on the primary trail placing third in popular vote; his performance in televised debates; his visit to Central America, and his major address to the nation at the Democratic national convention.

The Jackson campaign was important because it raised progressive issues in a national campaign. Without Jackson's campaign efforts, whole segments of society would have been systematically eliminated from electoral participation. Jackson increased the number of registered black voters throughout the country, and his campaign gave hope to many people who had lost faith in the American political system. He spoke out against the Democratic party's drift toward conservatism, and he was the only Democratic leader to denounce Reagan's surprise military attack on Libya.

Jackson continued his quest to institutionalize the struggle for social justice within the context of presidential politics. For those analysts who thought the Jackson campaign was a one-shot burning star that would burn out later, Jackson came back for the 1988 presidential election with even more spirit than he demonstrated in 1984. He broadened his coalition to include white middle-Americans as Jackson became the most dynamic spokesperson on the drug issue, economic issues relating to working men and women, economic justice, and work conditions for average Americans. As Jackson's white support increased and as his opponents dropped out of the race one by one, Jackson's huge media coverage increased even more dramatically. In the end, Jackson finished a strong second to Michael Dukakis in the delegate count at the Democratic National Convention in 1988, and put himself in a position where he could exact certain concessions from the Democratic party.

After Jackson's defeat, his political activism reached new heights. He adopted tactics of the Southern Christian Leadership Conference (SCLC) and brought them north to Chicago, Illinois, to supervise "Operation Breadbasket." After a falling-out with SCLC leadership, the brash young Jackson formed his own civil rights group called "People United to Save Humanity" or PUSH. He continued to organize and politicize his constituencies in Chicago by turning to economic issues that hurt people. He organized economic boycotts against companies that had higher prices in ghetto stores as compared to their suburban stores and worked for more minority hirings in all fields.

Jackson became a strong fixture on the television and lecture circuit. He appeared at major rallies and was a most sought-after speaker. As definitive confirmation of his celebrity status, he even made the front page of the *National Enquirer* in 2001 when he admitted he had fathered a child out of wedlock with a woman who had worked for his organization.[19]

However, the celebrity presidency media movement that propelled figures like Jackson and Reagan to the forefront was not without its setbacks. With the decline of communism in 1990, the American presidency changed dramatically thereafter. The democratic movement spread to East Germany, Romania, Czechoslovakia, Hungary, and throughout most of the Warsaw Pact countries and the Soviet Union. The end of the Cold War presented the American presidency with a new set of leadership and communication challenges.

The presidency in the 1990s faced three imperatives according to Richard Rose:

> [T]o exercise influence within a system of separated powers, a President must "go Washington," that is, learn how to bargain with Congressmen, bureaucrats, and interest groups who can make or break his policy initiatives. "Going public" is a second imperative; after an arduous campaign for election the President must continue campaigning for popular support for himself and his policies. "Going international" is the third imperative, involving bargaining with foreigners about matters of economic and national security policy.[20]

Part of the challenge of going public in the post–Cold War era was figuring out how to use the media and the infrastructure of celebrity politics to maintain support for the presidency. If communism no longer presented a monolithic, interventionist, ideological challenge to American democracy, then how could the country keep the presidency at the center of "crisis" and the television show?[21]

With the collapse of communism, the president was called upon to solve many domestic problems that were deferred or ignored in the 1980s. President George Bush responded like many other American presidents, lapsing into a macho style that took full advantage of celebrity politics.[22] One thing Bush did was to anoint himself as a competitive fighter in various media accounts. If the presidential contest is like the Super Bowl of American politics, then Vince Lombardi's dictate describes presidential politics, "Winning isn't everything. It's the only thing." On the competitive continuum, Bush was almost off the scale for his overcompetitiveness. One would have to go back to Kennedy to find a president as competitive as Bush.

During the 1988 presidential campaign, the major media went so far as to ask the question, "Is George Bush a Wimp?" After the media confrontation with Dan Rather who questioned Bush live on CBS news about Bush's involvement with the Iran–Contra scandal, Bush demonstrated his overcompetitive presidential style. According to Bob Schieffer and Gary Gates, Bush's media advisor stationed himself next to the camera and wrote out key responses on a legal pad so that Bush could give the correct response and so that Bush would know when to publicly attack Dan Rather over his own anchoring problems.[23] Bush quickly exited the studio after his live performance and told reporters that Rather was a "pussy." Bush bragged to his aides that

Rather was a bastard who "didn't lay a glove on me." Moreover, Bush claimed that he should have received "combat pay" for his media performance with Rather. The next day, the Bush campaign issued a statement that said Mr. Bush had actually called Mr. Rather a "pussycat" rather than the reported "pussy." After this exchange, the major media pronounced that Bush was no longer a wimp. After that point, virtually no reporter questioned Bush about his role in the Iran–Contra scandal.[24]

Taking advantage of media interest in human feature aspects of the presidency, Bush made extensive use of sporting activities during his time in the White House. He loved sports competition and the organized sports system in the United States. Bush played tennis at least once a week, he ran about three times a week, and he worked out on exercise equipment. He enjoyed watching football, basketball, and baseball as well as other sports. He shot baskets once in a while, and he loved fishing. Bush enjoyed playing golf whenever he had time, and he was reported to play eighteen holes of golf in less than two hours! In 1989 Bush participated in twenty-three different sports ranging from volleyball to horseshoes.[25]

President Bush liked to invite the press corps to watch him participate in his sporting outings. Bush's fishing friends called the president "Coach," and Bush liked to refer to himself as "Mr. Smooth" when he played tennis and golf. Bush loved to play tennis on the White House courts. He did not micromanage the tennis courts to decide who got to use the "ultimate tennis club," but he kept track of wins and losses. According to Marlin Fitzwater, Bush considered how a person played tennis to be a good indicator of character. Fitzwater said, "The President judges people by their competitive attitude on the court. He likes people who are competitive as well as fun."[26]

Bush was noted for organizing competitive doubles matches in tennis in which the president took the visiting celebrity professional tennis player as his partner. Bush ambushed his opponents with the likes of Bjorn Borg and Pete Sampras as one-time playing partners. During the Sampras tennis outing, Bush and Sampras played as a team for two hours and defeated Marvin Bush and one of his friends. Sampras commented, "When we won, that made [Bush's day]. We played for two hours. He wanted to play more, but I had to stop so I could visit relatives."[27]

Indeed, Bush framed himself as the nation's number-one sports fan. Expanding on the tradition started by Richard Nixon of calling winning sports teams and personalities immediately after their nationally televised victories, Bush called almost everyone. He called winners of the World Series, the Super Bowl, the NBA Championships, the NCAA football winners, the NCAA basketball winners in the Division I Men's competition, and even the winner of the Indianapolis 500 race. He invited the winners to visit him at the White House for a visit and photo opportunities.

In foreign policy, the president made sure his actions were interpreted in a good-versus-evil framework. For example, while Bush was organizing his fragile international coalition against Saddam Hussein's invasion of Kuwait, White House media releases portrayed Hussein as an evil villain, similar to the way Hitler was discussed during World War II and the way a series of communist leaders had been treated during the Cold War. The prewar rhetoric more closely resembled the rhetoric coming from the hype of a heavyweight boxing match or of a World Wrestling Federation contest. The president's prewar macho posturing reached its peak on December 20, 1990, when Bush said, "If we get into an armed situation [Saddam is] going to get his ass kicked."[28] The framing paid off. Following the successful conclusion of the Gulf War, Bush's popularity was recorded at 89 percent by the Gallup organization, the highest rating of any American president in the history of polling. However, after the Gulf War, a declining economy and increasing national deficits eroded Bush's popularity and resulted in his defeat in the 1992 election.

After he defeated Bush in the 1992 election, President Bill Clinton got few breaks from the personalistic and aggressive style of tabloid journalism during his administration. Reflecting the tendency during this period to ask probing and highly personal questions of political leaders, such as whether he wore boxers or briefs (the answer was briefs), *Time* magazine trumpeted Clinton as "The Incredible Shrinking President."[29] Reporters wanted to know what Bill Clinton said, thought, felt, and did, past, present, and future. The president was the star and much press coverage focused on the "who, what, when, where, why, and how" for each presidential situation.

This focus on the president's personality inevitably reinforced the notion of the president as a major celebrity. The press did not focus on pragmatic calculations, bureaucratic politics, or institutional explanations of behavior. Instead, everything was explained in terms of the personality of the celebrity. *New York Times* reporter Michiko Kakutani characterized him as the "first user-friendly chief executive." At the 2000 White House Correspondents Association dinner, Clinton broadcast a video showing him being an ordinary guy whose every action should be of interest to the press—"buying smoked hams on eBay, doing his laundry, clipping the Rose Garden hedges, watching television with his dog, and running after Hillary's limousine with a brown-bag lunch."[30] The president himself defended the downsizing of the presidency by saying his goal was "to demystify the job."[31]

At the beginning of his term, Clinton had started with far-higher hopes. He had turned his mediated image from that "dope smoking, draft dodging, bimbo drilling bubba" of the campaign into the next coming of John F. Kennedy.[32] But Clinton's roller coaster ride over the next eight years would make his election coverage look like smooth sailing. At the beginning of his administration, Clinton had four days of inaugural festivities. Over 30 million people watched a preinaugural concert, "Call for Reunion," on Sunday, January 17, before the inauguration. As John Cooke noted, "Power attracts power. Last night when Clinton came to the inaugural ball, the most powerful people in Hollywood were lined up against the railing waiting to shake his hand. No matter how long it took."[33] Clinton played saxophone at the Arkansas Ball and hobnobbed with more celebrities than on Oscar night.

Clinton cultivated close ties with a long series of Hollywood actors. Judy Collins and later Barbra Streisand spent the night at the White House in spring of 1993, when they were invited by the Clintons. Actors Christopher Reeve, Richard Dreyfus, John Ritter, and Lindsay Wagner visited the Oval Office and during a visit to Vancouver for a summit, Clinton found time to visit Sharon Stone, Richard Gere, and Cindy Crawford.[34] By May 1993, Clinton had to defend himself against charges that his $200 haircut from Beverly Hills stylist Cristophe showed that Clinton no longer remembered the middle class. He went on *CBS This Morning* to tell Paula Zahn that he had not "gone Hollywood."[35]

The president responded to press complaints by broadening his celebrity worship. On June 20, 1993, he attended the first national celebration of "our country's sports legends." Clinton invited Kareem Abdul-Jabbar, Muhammad Ali, Arnold Palmer, and Ted Williams to the White House. This was taped as an NBC special. In September 1993, Bill and Hillary Rodham Clinton had dinner at the White House with Julia Roberts and her new husband, Lyle Lovett.[36]

By the 1996 election, celebrities rushed to line up either with Clinton or Dole, depending on their party leanings. The Republicans were represented by celebrity politicos, Arnold Schwarzenegger, Bruce Willis, Charlton Heston, Kelsey Grammer, and Rush Limbaugh. Democrats were represented by Steven Spielberg, Paul Newman, Stephen Stills, Sarah Jessica Parker, Dustin Hoffman, Barbra Streisand, Sharon Stone, Whoopi Goldberg, Robin Williams, Tom Hanks, Rob Reiner, Kevin Costner, Sally Field, and Roseanne.

Many of these entertainers gave large sums of money to Clinton. David Geffen gave $575,697 to Democratic efforts while his partners Steven Spielberg and Jeffrey Katzenberg donated $503,123 and $408,320 respectively to Democrats. Barbra Streisand contributed $142,825 and Don Henley gave $107,685 to the Democrats. Paul Newman donated $72,500 to Democrats. Tom Hanks emceed a Democratic fund-raiser in L.A. that featured Don Henley, Barbra Streisand, Maya Angelou, David Geffen, and others.[37] There was little question that Hollywood was in full support of many of Clinton's policies.

When the 1996 election was over, Clinton had won a second term handily over GOP nominee Bob Dole. However, if Clinton's first term had its ups and downs, the second term gyrated much more wildly. The rise of scandal coverage reached its ultimately frenzy in January 1998, when Internet Web master Matt Drudge revealed that Clinton had engaged in a sexual affair with a White House intern named Monica Lewinsky. Through the persistent efforts of independent prosecutor Ken Starr, the president's sex life, both past and present, became the focus of intense national media scrutiny.

In the process, the celebrity presidency evolved into its natural successor, the tabloid presidency. Political scandal became interchangeable with

Hollywood gossip. It was the logical culmination of changes in the media, shifts in the audience, and alterations in the political process. The nation had been forewarned about Clinton character problems through stories involving Gennifer Flowers, Paula Jones, the draft, smoking marijuana, Whitewater, Travelgate, Filegate, and illegal campaign contributions.

But no one could have predicted that Clinton would have an extramarital affair with a young White House intern. Even satirical movies like *Primary Colors* with John Travolta as a Clinton-type president and *Wag the Dog* with Dustin Hoffman were superseded by real-life events in the Clinton presidency. The national media reported the down and dirty details of the sexual affair as they became available. The political humor and satire against Clinton reached its zenith during the Year of Monica. Clinton's presidency was reduced to a series of sex jokes by late-night comedians, David Letterman, Jay Leno, Conan O'Brien, and Bill Maher that centered around oral sex and Clinton's libido.

The following were among the Clinton jokes that circulated over the Internet:

1. What is the definition of an Arkansas virgin? A girl that can run faster than the governor.
2. Clinton is taking his JFK image thing a little too far. Recently he bought a Marilyn Monroe stamp and licked the wrong side.
3. A Clinton aide rushed into the Oval Office and asked the president what the administration's position on the new abortion bill should be. Clinton replied, "Just go ahead and pay it."
4. What does Clinton mean by safe sex? When Hillary is out of town.

Eventually, Clinton was impeached by the House, but won the resulting removal trial in the Senate. Much to the surprise of many, rather than turning on Clinton, citizens blamed overzealous Republicans and reporters for the national trauma. The president's poll numbers remained quite high, except for rankings of his trust and integrity.

By the time he left office, Clinton had the highest job performance ratings (66 percent) of any president in the post–World War II period (beating Reagan by a few percentage points). Although it at times seemed dazed by the ebbs and flows of the Clinton presidency, the public appreciated Clinton's persistence, the good economy, and his excellent communications skills. His personalization of the office had contributed to the strong connection that many Americans felt toward the former Arkansas governor. However, his controversial pardons of fugitive financier Marc Rich and several cocaine dealers during his last days in office ignited a firestorm of protests over the wisdom of the moves. As a former president, it was no surprise that Clinton provoked the same degree of controversy as he had during his actual term of office.

At the turn of the millennium, it was apparent that the fall of the Soviet Union and the end of the Cold War had produced major changes in American life. By eliminating the national security threat of thermonuclear war and without an evil empire to keep the Cold War, bipartisan nuclear consensus together, the stability of the American political system collapsed. New domestic and economic issues became paramount, and politicians and citizens were free to focus on issues of health care, the environment, the economy, taxes, government regulation, education, crime, drugs, and abortion. Without the cohesiveness provided by an all-powerful enemy like the Soviet Union, the new challenge became *internal threats*.

Furthermore, shifts in our means of mass communications have altered the American system. The explosion of cable, the proliferation of 24-hour news channels, the Internet, tabloids, conservative talk radio, stand-up political comedians, news magazines, political movies about imagined presidential behavior, and the tabloidization of the mainstream news outlets has altered the situation radically. In the crass, crude discourse of the contemporary period, which included the Nancy and Tonya story, the O. J. Simpson story, and the sinful sportscasters Frank Gifford and Marv Albert, the story of the 1990s was about the President having sex with a White House intern.

Throughout the episode, Americans watched the public drama on television. The evening news became just another form of entertainment.[38] The political celebrities and celebrity politicos were a cast of entertaining characters in the drama. As Orrin Klapp has observed, there are many kinds of different symbolic leaders to choose from.[39] However, all the choices involve someone who is famous, who has been made into a celebrity, and who is celebrated in public by the media. Citizens have the power to select the kinds of heroes and role models that they want, but more often than not, mass media promotes certain role models over others.[40]

When George W. Bush was elected president in 2000, it seemed the perfect culmination to the era of celebrity politics. A classic legacy candidate, Bush both embraced and benefited from celebrity status. His presidential run was aided enormously by his family's connections. As the first $100 million president in terms of campaign fund-raising, Bush jumped to the forefront of the GOP and beat Al Gore, a sitting vice president campaigning with the benefit of a strong economy. It was a victory that was both surprising, yet perfectly predictable given broader changes that had taken place in American politics.

However, similar to Clinton, Bush suffered from tabloid coverage and probes into his early adulthood. He admitted he had "made mistakes" in his youth. Observers speculated about drug use early in life; it was revealed late in the campaign that he had been arrested for driving under the influence of alcohol in 1976. When reporters pressed him to talk specifically about his misbehavior, Bush laughed them off as "youthful indiscretions" and refused to provide any additional details to the press.

Satirists ridiculed Bush for not being smart and riding the coattails of his family name. Jay Leno, for example, joked that Bush "is relieved that the whole DUI incident has become known because it's 'you know, maybe they'll get off my back about the cocaine thing'" and proclaimed Bush as "the man who put the party back in Republican party."[41] These kinds of comments were a classic way to belittle a legacy candidate. As with Ted Kennedy, Patrick Kennedy, and other children of famous politicians, the insinuation was that the person's meteoric rise in U.S. politics was due to ascribed status and family name more than demonstrated accomplishments. Bush was an empty suit, critics claimed. It was a subtle way to remind the public that this type of celebrity politics remained alive and well in the United States, in both good and bad ways.

At George W. Bush's inauguration, the new president invited Latin singer Ricky Martin to sing as the opening act. Thousands thronged to the event, which also featured Las Vegas performer Wayne Newton and Christian entertainer Sandi Patti singing the national anthem. One young person in attendance conceded, "I don't know nothing about government. But I know Ricky Martin is here, and it's free. If Bush is letting us see Ricky, then I like Bush."[42]

With media bringing the entertaining public drama to citizens, the values of show business become the important values for political success. The government becomes a "superstar show."[43] Political reporters become entertainment and gossip reporters. Political success is measured in public opinion polls and media success is measured in ratings. The "dimensions of political drama" need celebrities to communicate the play.[44]

These entertainment values of mass media news create a mediated political reality for citizens.[45] The problems of living in a democracy where entertainment is the most important goal has been well-documented previously. Norman Corwin was one of the first social commentators to call attention to this extraordinary change in American public life when he wrote *Trivializing America: The Triumph of Mediocrity*.[46]

Neil Postman continued the analysis by observing that American citizens were overamused. In *Amusing Ourselves to Death: Public Discourse in the Age of Show Business*, Postman details how our civic discourse has been degraded by contemporary changes in our process.[47] Paul Slansky covered the problem better than any other social critic by compiling major news stories to show what kinds of news stories were deemed important in the American celebrity political culture. His book, *The Clothes Have No Emperor: A Chronicle of the American '80s* presented a shocking indictment of the kind of celebrity gossip society we have become.[48] Its popularity demonstrated how the celebrity regime both elevates fame and sometimes turns harshly on its prominent subjects.

NOTES

1. Darrell M. West, *The Rise and Fall of the Media Establishment* (Boston: Bedford/St. Martin's Press, 2001), pp. 64–65.

2. Darrell M. West, *The Rise and Fall of the Media Establishment* (Boston: Bedford/St. Martin's Press, 2001), pp. 58–59.

3. John Dimmick and Thomas Cain, eds. "Use of Mass Media," *American Behavioral Scientist* 23, no. 1 (September/October 1979).

4. Mihaly Csikszentmihalyi and Robert Kobey, "Television and the Rest of Life," *Public Opinion Quarterly* 45 (fall 1981), pp. 317–328.

5. *Minneapolis Star Tribune*, "Richard M. Nixon: A Respectable Cloth Coat and a Dog Named Checkers," 30 October 2000, p. 11-A.

6. Seymour Hersh, *The Dark Side of Camelot* (New York: Little, Brown, 1997).

7. Neil Postman, *Amusing Ourselves to Death: Public Discourse in the Age of Show Business* (New York: Viking Penguin, 1986).

8. Norman Corwin, *Trivializing America: The Triumph of Mediocrity* (New York: Lyle Stuart, 1986).

9. Ron Nesson, "Too Much Trivia, Too Little Substance," *TV Guide*, 12–18 March 1979, pp. 2–6.

10. David Rosenbloom, *The Election Men* (New York: Quadrangle Books, 1973).

11. John J. O'Connor, "As an Exploiter of TV, the President Is Masterful," *New York Times*, 5 June 1983, p. H-27.

12. John Orman, *Comparing Presidential Behavior* (Westport, CT: Greenwood Press, 1987) pp. 152, 163.

13. Haynes Johnson, "It Was Wrong to Exclude the Press from the Grenada Invasion," *Washington Post Weekly Edition*, 14 November 1983, p. 29 and Drew Middleton, "Baring Reporters from the Battlefield," *New York Times Magazine*, 5 February 1984, pp. 36–37.

14. Mark Green and Gail MacColl, *There He Goes Again: Ronald Reagan's Reign of Error* (New York: Pantheon, 1983).

15. Jeff Colon, "The Press Slept while Reagan Rambled," www.fair.org/articles/reagan-press.html, February 7, 1999.

16. "Average Number of Press Conferences per Year," *Time*, 30 March 1987, p. 23.

17. John Orman, *Presidential Accountability* (Westport, CT: Greenwood Press, 1990), p. 51.

18. Tom Bower, "Was the Bombing of Tripoli a Misguided Vendetta by Reagan?" *The Listener*, 2 April 1987, p. 4.

19. Howard Kurtz, "Tabloid News Again Floods the Mainstream," *Washington Post*, 19 January 2001, p. C-1.

20. Richard Rose, "The Post-Modern Presidency: The World Closes in on the White House," *Presidency Research* X, no. 2 (spring 1988), p. 8 and his *The Post Modern President* (New Jersey: Chatham House, 1988) and Ryan Barilleaux, "Post-Modern American Presidency," *Presidency Research* X, no. 1 (fall 1987), pp. 15–18.

21. See Thomas Friedman, "Police Work: Hanging Tough Won't Be the Only Test of Leadership," *New York Times*, 19 August 1990, section 4, p. 1; John Mearsheimer, "Why We Will Soon Miss the Cold War," *The Atlantic Monthly*, August 1990, pp. 35–50; and John Lukacs, "The Stirrings of History: A New World Rises from the Ruins of Empire," *Harper's Magazine*, August 1990, pp. 41–48.

22. John Orman, *Comparing Presidential Behavior: Carter, Reagan, and the Macho Presidential Style* (Westport, CT: Greenwood Press, 1987), pp. 7–8.

23. Bob Schieffer and Gary Gates, "That Bush–Rather Blowup: A New Twist," *TV Guide*, 8–14 July 1989, p. 35.

24. Sidney Blumenthal, *Pledging Allegiance: The Last Campaign of the Cold War* (New York: Harper Collins, 1990), p. 75.

25. Hugh Sidey, "Totaling Up One Year," *Time*, 5 February 1990, p. 23.

26. Maureen Dowd, "The Ultimate Tennis Club," *Sports Illustrated*, 15 October 1990, p. 9.

27. "Sampras–Bush Ticket," *USA Today*, 4 October 1990, p. 11-C.

28. Jessica Lee, "Frustrated Bush Renews Threat of Force," *USA Today*, 21 December 1990, p. 1.

29. Michiko Kakutani, "With the Guy Next Door in the Oval Office, the Presidency Shrinks Further," *New York Times*, 19 January 2001, p. A-17.

30. Michiko Kakutani, "With the Guy Next Door in the Oval Office, the Presidency Shrinks Further," *New York Times*, 19 January 2001, p. A-17.

31. Michiko Kakutani, "With the Guy Next Door in the Oval Office, the Presidency Shrinks Further," *New York Times*, 19 January 2001, p. A-17.

32. Ken Auletta, "How the Politicians and the Public Stopped Reading Newspapers and Listening to Sam Donaldson and Learned to Loathe the Media: An Election Year Anatomy of an Institution in Decline," *Esquire*, November 1991, p. 107.

33. Bernard Weintraub, "Hollywood Crowd Gives Capital Two Thumbs Up," *New York Times*, 20 January 1995, p. A-15.

34. *Newsweek*, "Bel Air on the Potomac," 26 April 1993, p. 7.

35. Bill Nichols, "Clinton's Ire Zeroes in on Familiar Target: The Press," *USA Today*, 28 May 1993, p. 8-A.

36. Jeannie Williams, "The Lovetts Drop in on Bill and Hill," *USA Today*, 14 September 1993, p. 2-D.

37. *USA Today*, "Celebs Political Cash Flow," 26 August 1996, p. 2-D.

38. See Daniel Hallin, "Network News," in *Watching Television*, ed. Todd Gitlin (New York: Pantheon, 1986), pp. 9–41 and Leo Bogart, "Television News as Entertainment," in *The Entertainment Functions of Television*, ed. Percy H. Tannenbaum (Hillsdale, NJ: Lawrence Erlbaum Publishers, 1980), pp. 209–250.

39. Orrin Klapp, *Symbolic Leaders* (Chicago: Aldine Publishing, 1964).

40. Mark Gerzon, *A Choice of Heroes* (Boston: Houghton Mifflin, 1982).

41. Quoted on the Center for Media and Political Affairs Web site, www.cmpa.com, January 24, 2001.

42. Carol Morello, "Warming Up the Crowd," *Washington Post*, 19 January 2001, p. B-1.

43. Roger-Gerard Schwartzenberg, *The Superstar Show of Government* (Woodbury, NY: Barron's, 1980).

44. James Combs, *Dimensions of Political Drama* (Santa Monica, CA: Goodyear Publishing, 1980) and James Combs, *POLPOP* (Bowling Green, OH: Bowling Green University Popular Press, 1984).

45. See Dan Nimmo and James Combs, *Mediated Political Realities* (New York and London: Longman, 1983) and Dan Nimmo and James Combs, *Subliminal Politics* (Englewood Cliffs, NJ: Prentice Hall, 1980).

46. Norman Corwin, *Trivializing America* (Secaucus, NJ: Lyle Stuart, 1986).

47. Neil Postman, *Amusing Ourselves to Death: Public Discourse in the Age of Show Business* (New York: Penguin, 1986).

48. Paul Slansky, *The Clothes Have No Emperor: A Chronicle of the American '80s* (New York: Simon & Schuster, 1989).

ACTIVIST CELEBRITIES

America's love affair with the motion picture has never faltered. The magic of Hollywood has been an important centerpiece to American popular culture. Movies act as political socializing agents as they help citizens to understand the filmmakers worldview about the country's political system. Movies teach us how to act by showing us fantasies and stereotypes from the world of the filmmaker. The "reality" on the big screen (and now available on videocassette and DVD) often has an impact on viewers that is greater than the mediated political reality from television news.

The movie *Dr. Strangelove* demonstrated the crazy logic of nuclear deterrence in the Cold War period. *The Deerhunter* showed the haunting aftermath of the Vietnam War. Steven Spielberg's film *Saving Private Ryan* with Tom Hanks revealed the randomness of death during the Normandy Beach invasion in World War II. The movie *9 to 5* portrayed the travails of working women through the eyes of Dolly Parton, Jane Fonda, and Lily Tomlin.

From the beginning, Hollywood movie executives have kept their eye on Washington politics to make sure that the film industry did not become over-regulated or the subject of witch-hunts, as happened during the 1950s. Movies have become big business within the United States and a major export to foreign countries. Consumers spent $11.4 billion in 2000 going to one of the 37,000 movie screens that exist in North America. Leading films raise hundreds of millions of dollars for their producers.[1]

One of the first influential Hollywood moguls to become interested in national politics was Louis B. Mayer. He concentrated his energies on pursuing a friendship with President Herbert Hoover and on trying to recruit other celebrities toward supporting Hoover. During the Great Depression of the 1930s, many young Hollywood celebrities rebelled against their conservative bosses who supported Republicans. The new film stars like Katharine Hepburn, Orson Welles, Melvyn Douglas, and Ronald Reagan supported Franklin D. Roosevelt in his efforts to ease the burden on the downtrodden.[2]

After World War II, a conservative tide swept over Hollywood. During the communist scares of 1947–1953, many Hollywood celebrity politicos became the target of Washington's paranoia about spies. Senator Joseph McCarthy saw communists everywhere and especially in the Hollywood film community. Due to McCarthyism, many former Hollywood celebrity politicos found themselves on industry blacklists.[3] Among these were Charlie Chaplin, John Randolph, and Sterling Hayden to name a few of the more than 250 persons blacklisted in Hollywood. These individuals were utterly unable to get acting or writing jobs for a number of years. In many cases, they were forced to seek other kinds of employment or to leave the country.[4]

First as a young Republican representative on the House Committee on Un-American Activities and then as a senatorial candidate, Richard Nixon trashed Hollywood liberals and engaged in "red-baiting." In 1947 Nixon voted to subpoena the "Hollywood Ten" to bring them to Washington to question their leftist backgrounds. In 1948 Nixon attacked Hollywood liberals who supported progressive Henry Wallace's campaign for the presidency as a third party. Then in 1950 Nixon unmercifully attacked actress Helen Gahagen Douglas as a pink lady in his victorious U.S. Senate campaign in California.[5]

It was not until the glamorous years of the Kennedy administration in the early 1960s that many celebrity politicos in Hollywood felt safe to resume high-visibility politicking. Kennedy received support from Frank Sinatra, brother-in-law Peter Lawford, Henry Fonda, Melvyn Douglas, Janet Leigh, Angie Dickinson, Gene Kelly, and many others. Kennedy operated the American presidency as if he were a Hollywood matinee idol himself. He developed friendly relations with Judy Garland, Tony Curtis, Lauren Bacall, Shirley MacLaine, and Milton Berle. Most of the Hollywood political celebrities supported the Kennedy administration as Washington and Hollywood seemed to come together in the early 1960s. Perhaps the ultimate Hollywood–Washington connection came in the close personal relationship that developed between Jack Kennedy and Marilyn Monroe.

In the late 1960s and early 1970s, more celebrity politicos from Hollywood scored big in American popular culture as antiwar activists. The war in Vietnam developed a strong backlash in public opinion from 1967 to 1971 and many celebrities who had once supported Lyndon Johnson's earlier efforts to defend South Vietnam turned their political energies to opposing the war in Indochina. In 1968, Robert Vaughn worked long hours in the "Dump LBJ" movement, and celebrities Paul Newman, Tony Randall, Myrna Loy, and Leonard Nimoy labored on behalf of the Eugene McCarthy campaign in New Hampshire. By the late 1960s and early 1970s, actress Jane Fonda had become the darling of the antiwar movement, and a symbol of national rebellion, although ultimately her peace efforts would produce a major backlash from angry veterans organizations.

In the 1970s, actor Warren Beatty became the great organizer of celebrities to campaign for George McGovern in the 1972 presidential election. This action helped to institutionalize the formal role of celebrity coordinator in election campaigns. During the late 1960s and early 1970s, conservatives like John Wayne came to symbolize support for LBJ and Richard Nixon's Vietnam War policies from old Hollywood. By 1980, the Hollywood backlash was completed in conservative style with the ultimate celebrity political participation in the U.S. political system, Ronald Reagan's presidential campaign. With Reagan's victories in 1980 and 1984, the conservative trend of old Hollywood, as seen in the celebrity backing, came to dominate Hollywood celebrity politics until the progressive resurgence of young Hollywood in the late 1980s around a series of pressing policy issues.

American politics also has been profoundly influenced by the entertainment art form known as popular music. Popular music provides the background for political candidates who want to sell images to the voting public, such as Clinton's use of Fleetwood Mac lyrics and Reagan's reliance on Lee Greenwood's song, "I'm Proud to Be an American."

Popular music has pervaded many other aspects of American society as well. Rock music fills the air in the domed playgrounds of the professional sports teams, and popular music is a necessary attraction to sell plays and motion pictures.

American popular music has even had some major impact in terms of the profound global changes that have occurred over the past few years. Indeed, some analysts have observed that the collapse of the Eastern European bloc countries and, indeed, the collapse of the Soviet political economy itself, was not so much the failure of Marxist systems, but rather it was the inability of these systems to deliver Big Macs, Levis, and rock music to its young people to keep them entertained and out of the street demonstrations against the regime. Karl Marx in his political theory never anticipated the problem that "I want my MTV" could create for decision makers in socialist countries.[6]

Yet as popular music has acted as a subversive instrument in some socialist states to help bring about more democratic freedoms, ironically, in the United States, popular music has been at the center of controversy for those who want to limit artistic expression and rights of consumers to buy what they want to buy. Certain rap artists and heavy metal rockers have become the target of censors who want to forbid certain words, expressions, and actions from being performed, such as restrictions proposed by Tipper Gore in the 1980s. Citizens groups organized to fight certain forms of popular music, and this follows the tradition established over the past four decades of popular music in America where organized crackdowns against popular music appear about once every ten years.

With the huge success of popular music in America and around the globe in the 1990s, it is no surprise that a new network known as MTV married the lyrics of music with the visual aspects of television. Previously, one could listen to music and conjure up images in one's head about what the song was supposed to be about. Every mind had its own image system that would run individual images of a rock song into the listener's consciousness. After MTV, the video played on television is a visual image that is implanted in people's imagination whenever the song or lyric is played. The video stimulation became more important in many respects than the actual spoken words of the music.

In many respects, celebrity activists from the fields of acting and music represent the perfect combination of Hollywood, Washington, and the mass media. News executives love to incorporate prominent celebrities in their shows because of the attention that is drawn to the event. In 2000, for example, Phil Griffin, the executive producer of *Hardball*, booked actress Goldie Hawn on the show after she attended a press conference demanding that Congress vote about a China trade bill. When asked when he invited her to be a guest on the talk show, Griffin noted that "the China trade deal ain't exactly a big winner on these talk shows, or anywhere, for that matter, so I said, 'Let's get her on.'"[7] It was a way to draw attention to a subject that normally does not elicit much public interest.

The Washington bureau chief for Fox News Channel viewed the growing trend of famous celebrity activists appearing on television shows to lobby government officials as mutually advantageous. "We probably have three or four celebrities appear on Capitol Hill a week," Kim Hume said. "Granted, I'm sure there are celebrities who have real passion about particular issues and they really do want to make a difference. But most of it is a collusion between the way they wish the public would see them and the way the public relations people use them in order to get attention for their causes."[8]

In the profiles that follow, we examine some of the more important Hollywood celebrities and rock stars who have directed their stardom toward political causes. Through these case studies, we show what kinds of issues attract the attention of entertainment performers and what kinds of reactions they have generated from the media and the political community. As will be apparent, these Hollywood celebrities have become an increasingly important part of our national debate over policy issues.

HOLLYWOOD CELEBRITIES

MARLON BRANDO

One of the great American movie actors, Marlon Brando, has been a long-time political activist who has remained true to his worldview. As early as 1949, Brando took part in demonstrations for the political and social rights of minorities. Along with his close friend, singer and celebrity Harry Belafonte,

Brando took part in many of the major civil rights protests from 1961 to 1963. In March 1963, he demonstrated in Maryland because of the brutal treatment given black Americans by the state national guard.

In July 1963, Brando took part in a major demonstration sponsored by the Congress of Racial Equality in Los Angeles to protest discriminatory housing policy. In August 1963, Brando went with James Baldwin and Harry Belafonte to attend Dr. Martin Luther King, Jr.'s "Great March on Washington." He also participated in a protest meeting held by American Civil Liberties Union, Congress of Racial Equality, and the National Association for the Advancement of Colored People to bring attention to racism in Hollywood, including racist stereotyping in movies and the lack of movie roles for black actors.[9]

In 1966, Brando turned his activist attention toward famine in India. He began raising money, and he made large personal contributions to the United Nations International Children's Education Fund for famine relief. Brando believed that human suffering anywhere in the world should be eased, and that Americans should not ignore the sufferings of other people because of the color of their skin. In April 1968, Brando, like other Americans, was distraught over the assassination of Dr. Martin Luther King, Jr. Brando pledged 12 percent of his earnings to Dr. King's organizational base for the civil rights movement, the Southern Christian Leadership Conference. In May 1968, Brando walked with New York mayor, John Lindsay, in Harlem to promote racial brotherhood. In June of that year, Brando attended a funeral of a Black Panther party member and promised to continue fighting against racism in the United States.

In the early 1970s Brando worked with Dennis Banks and Russell Means to help form the American Indian Movement. Brando began working hard in his social activism to redress the injustices that were perpetuated on Native Americans. While Brando was at Wounded Knee, South Dakota, with the Oglala Sioux Indians protesting housing and job discrimination against the tribe, he sent Native American Sasheen Littlefeather to the Academy Award ceremonies in case he won the Oscar for Best Actor. Brando, indeed, won the award in 1973 for the movie *The Godfather*, and Ms. Littlefeather told a startled national audience that Brando refused to accept the Oscar because of the treatment of American Indians in film and in American history. In January 1974, Brando gave forty acres of his property to the Red Wind Association, which represented some twenty-three tribes, so that at least he could make some personal amends to Native Americans who had their land stolen by the white men.

In recent years, Brando has marched with Jesse Jackson and other civil rights leaders to protest racism in Los Angeles and worked to dismantle apartheid in South Africa. He donated his salary and his profits from the antiapartheid movie *A Dry White Season*, which amounted to nearly $14 million, to the antiapartheid groups struggling for social, racial, and political justice in South Africa.

CHARLTON HESTON

The biggest draw among conservative audiences is Charlton Heston, the long-time actor and star of the classic movie *Ben Hur* and who played Moses in the *Ten Commandments*. A supporter of Ronald Reagan and Newt Gingrich, Heston was elected president of the National Rifle Association in 1998. Around the country, he took his message about the need to maintain the right to bear arms and the virtues of individuals being able to carry concealed weapons. Citing the thirty-one states that had passed pro-gun laws, Heston claimed "crime was diminished by about 50 percent."[10]

During the 2000 election, Heston embarked on a sixteen-city, get-out-the-vote drive designed to mobilize gun owners against Democrats who supported gun control. Appearing at one event in Nashville, Heston showed the closely intertwined nature of politics and acting when he started his speech by saying, "I've been a public performer most of my life, and I've never seen a crowd response like this. Ah, well, maybe at the Academy Awards." Asked why he was spending so much time on the road, Heston made a veiled reference to his celebrity status: "I can get people to come to a luncheon and pay a disgusting amount of money."[11] In a number of congressional races around the country, but especially in the South and West, Heston's efforts are thought to have provided major assistance to pro-gun candidates.

CLINT EASTWOOD

In the 1980s Clint Eastwood rose to political celebrity stardom. His movie one-liners like "Go, ahead. Make my day," became sound bites for President Ronald Reagan and other conservative politicians. In 1986 Eastwood decided to run for mayor of Carmel, California, and won. He served for two years and his name has been touted by political consultants from the right of the spectrum as an important celebrity politico because of his macho image and his tremendous name recognition.

Eastwood decided to run for the mayor of Carmel because the town government would not let the Hollywood star put up a new building next to his restaurant. After Eastwood threatened to sue the planning commission, the administration gave Eastwood approval to build. However, this snub by the town officials inspired Eastwood to run for mayor. In another dispute, land developers wanted to buy some property and put up a huge housing complex, but Eastwood spent over $5 million of his own money to keep developers out. He bought the property to preserve the nearby wetlands.

Eastwood was vocal as mayor of Carmel in speaking out against offshore oil drilling that would hurt the environment. For such a political conservative, the macho, lonesome cowboy turned into an environmentalist. He wanted to protect national parks and to clean up our air and water. Regardless of

Eastwood's environmental bent, Dirty Harry is still considered to be a top Republican celebrity because of his wealth, name recognition, and macho political style.[12]

In the early 1960s, Jane Fonda was known as the daughter of the famous actor Henry Fonda and as a sex symbol along the lines of an American Brigette Bardot. By the end of the 1960s, Fonda became the darling of the antiwar movement and a sex symbol for young male militants in much the same way that Angela Davis became such a symbol for the militant movement to end racism in the United States. The Hollywood star became the target of domestic surveillance and harassment by the government because of her political activism. Richard Nixon and Henry Kissinger used the FBI, the CIA, and the Defense Intelligence Agency to spy on Fonda's every word and move.

She started to become more political in her beliefs around 1968, when she learned how her brother, Peter Fonda, opposed the Vietnam War, even though it opened a political rift with her father. In 1970, Jane Fonda moved from disgusted citizen to antiwar-movement activist. Fonda's politicization began when she supported the takeover of Alcatraz Island by militant Native Americans in the fall of 1969. Fonda appeared at rallies and raised funds for the occupation of the former prison island.

The next group that Fonda openly supported was the Black Panther party as led by Huey Newton and Bobby Seale. Fonda began calling police and other authorities "pigs," and she closed her speeches with "Power to the people." At this point, Fonda turned all of her energies toward supporting the antiwar movement to end the war in Vietnam. She toured military coffeehouses near bases to provide entertainment and political diatribes on her infamous FTA tours (which meant either "Fuck or Free the Army"). She toured with Donald Sutherland, Dick Gregory, and Peter Boyle, with the goal of politicizing individual soldiers against the war.

Fonda participated in demonstrations all across the country against Vietnam, militarism, sexism, racism, and against genocide of Native Americans. She participated in the major marches on Washington, D.C., in 1970 and 1971. She spoke out against Nixon, the invasion of Cambodia, and the killing of demonstrators at Kent State University in 1970. She worked closely with the Vietnam Veterans Against the War organization as she tried to raise money for the group.[13]

By July 1972, Fonda had become, once and forever, "Hanoi Jane" in some circles as she visited North Vietnam. Fonda spoke out against the bombing of North Vietnam, she attacked American POW's who had dropped the bombs on Hanoi, and she attacked Nixon for his "war crimes." She broadcast a message to American soldiers telling them to stop fighting the North Vietnamese in the internal Vietnam civil war. Fonda had moved from militant antiwar spokesperson who wanted to stop the war to apologetic cheerleader for Ho Chi Minh and Le Duc Tu of North Vietnam.

In 2000, Fonda contributed $12 million to pro-choice groups to protect women's right to choose on abortion. This extraordinary contribution financed issue ads in a number of leading congressional races designed to boost public awareness of an abortion rights stance. Along with Oprah Winfrey, Glenn Close, Calista Flockhart, Ali MacGraw, and Winona Ryder, Fonda appeared in a major rally at Madison Square Garden protesting violence against women. One of the highlights of the event called "V-Day," was Fonda's performance in the Eve Ensler play, "The Vagina Monologues."[14] She also donated $12 million in 2001 to Harvard University to underwrite research on factors affecting the self-images of boys and girls.

PAUL NEWMAN AND JOANNE WOODWARD

Two of the most consistently principled celebrity politicos are Paul Newman and Joanne Woodward. Together they form a social activist team that raises funds for candidates who share their views, educates the public about various issues, sponsors fund-raisers for various political issues, and acts as media spokesperson for a number of important political issues. From the Great March on Washington, led by Dr. Martin Luther King, Jr., to the movement to end the nuclear arms race, Newman and Woodward have been there.

Newman and Woodward supported Dr. King through fund-raisers and appearances for the civil rights movement in 1963. In 1968 Paul Newman was a strong campaigner and organizer for Eugene McCarthy in an effort to get an anti–Vietnam War candidate elected. In the 1970s, Newman raised money for liberal candidates and Joanne Woodward began to raise money for the National Organization for Women to help the fight against sexism in the United States. Paul Newman became a proud member of Richard Nixon's "enemies list" in the early 1970s because of his liberal politics.

In the 1980s, both Newman and Woodward turned major energies toward ending the nuclear arms race. Paul Newman became a major spokesperson for the Nuclear Freeze movement and even debated Charlton Heston on ABC television as to the merits of freezing nuclear weapons production. Both remained active in charities like Newman's Own, which is supported by sales from Paul Newman food products, Save the Children Foundation, AIDS charities, and other local benefits in their Westport, Connecticut, neighborhood.

BARBRA STREISAND

Singer and Hollywood actress Barbra Streisand has devoted considerable time and energy raising money for Democrats and promoting liberal causes. As a young performer, she sang songs for President John Kennedy and Lyndon Johnson. She was a major supporter of George McGovern when he ran for president in 1972. In 2000, she hosted a $10 million fund-raiser for Clinton's Presidential Library and performed at a $1,000 per ticket Democratic National Committee fund-raiser following that party's nominating convention.

At that event, Streisand told the audience that "the first three reasons to vote for Al Gore are the Supreme Court, the Supreme Court, and the Supreme Court. Our whole way of life is at stake." She then explained her views on education, abortion, gun control, health care, and campaign finance reform. Commenting on her value to the party as an entertainment superstar, one Democratic official noted that "the average person pays about that much attention to politics (snapping her fingers), and she brings that much more attention to it. So I'm very grateful that she'll step out and say these issues are important to her."[15]

Following the election of President George W. Bush, Streisand wrote a three-page strategy memo to Capitol Hill Democrats exhorting them to attack the opposition. She began by posing the question, "What has happened to the Democrats since the November election? Some of you seem paralyzed, demoralized, and depressed." She concluded with some clear advice, "I hope you're through arguing among yourselves and distancing yourselves from President Clinton. . . . Let's not allow the Republicans to take away the gains we've made."[16] It was a sign of how closely integrated Hollywood stars had become with Washington politicians.

OPRAH WINFREY

Television personality, actress, and magazine publisher Oprah Winfrey has become the most popular talk show host in America. With a show that went on the air in 1986 and now reaches around seven million viewers every day, Winfrey has achieved the status of cultural icon. The premiere issue *O: The Oprah Magazine* sold over 1.6 million copies. Overall, her media empire is estimated at $725 million.[17]

Typically, she eschews politics on her television show, preferring instead to emphasize the personal and family issues of interest to her mostly female audience. But in 2000 for the first time, she invited actual candidates (Gore and Bush) in for hour-long interviews. Her explanation of the shift was that she hoped "to create the kind of environment and ask the questions that will allow us to break the political wall and see who each one is as a person."[18]

Gore made the first appearance and presented himself as loving family man who would fight for ordinary people. He explained his positions on issues such as education and health care, and talked about his wife and children. The visit allowed Gore to show a more human side of his often-stiff public personality.

However, Bush completely upstaged the vice president by planting a big kiss on Oprah's cheek when he walked out to greet her (as opposed to Gore's businesslike handshake with the host). One audience member asked what the greatest misconception was about him and Bush replied that it was the view that "I'm running on my daddy's name, that, you know, if my name were George Jones, I'd be a country and western singer." Bush then went on to discuss his favorite gift to give (a kiss to his wife), fast food (taco), sandwich (peanut butter and jelly on white bread), and historical figure (Winston Churchill).[19] The appearance was thought to have boosted Bush's fortunes and helped him among more moderate voters.

In keeping with her new spirit of political activism, Winfrey participated in a rally protesting violence against women. Her campaign contributions have gone exclusively to Democratic party committees.[20] But she has not formally endorsed any candidate for major office, due to her interest in not being seen as too partisan.

WARREN BEATTY

For many years, film star Warren Beatty has worked on behalf of a variety of liberal causes involving health insurance reform, campaign finance reform, and finding ways to connect citizens to politics. He has spoken out on these matters, contributed money, and written op-ed pieces explaining his opinions. He portrayed a populist senator in the movie *Bulworth*, and briefly considered running for president in 2000. Unhappy over the Democratic party's drift to the center during the Clinton years, Beatty contemplated a campaign after syndicated columnist Arianna Huffington broached the subject publicly. When asked about it, Beatty said, "It's not something I floated. But it is something I'm thinking about." This led California pollsters to include him in a state survey, which found that 44 percent each preferred Gore or Bush, while 8 percent favored Beatty.[21]

Although he ultimately decided not to run, the effort would have been consistent with his long-standing political activism. Beatty is considered one of the most active political fund-raisers in Hollywood and has maintained strong ties to the Democratic party establishment.

ROBERT REDFORD

Robert Redford also has established a long track record working for certain issues and candidates. In 1972, Robert Redford played in the movie *The Candidate*, which was supposed to point out the problems of superficial celebrity politics. It was a warning that was not heeded. The movie showed advance men, speechwriters, pollsters, hard-ball political advisors, and media consultants to be the real power brokers in the new American democracy. *The Candidate* showed how American politics has been overtaken by image consultants.

Redford supports environmental candidates who are sensitive to issues of energy conservation, wilderness protection, and antinuclear power. He has been active in national environmental conferences like the Clean Air conference in 1988. He openly supported Democrat Ted Wilson for the U.S. Senate in Utah, and he supported Gary Hart for president. He is known to have a strong distrust of professional politicians and prefers to work as a citizen activist.

ARNOLD SCHWARZENEGGER

One of the strongest conservative political celebrities is worldwide mega–film star Arnold Schwarzenegger. President George Bush liked to "hang" with Arnold and called him "Conan the Republican." Bush named Schwarzenegger as Chairman of the President's Council on Physical Fitness and Sports. Schwarzenegger has supported Pete Wilson of California, and he was a major backer of Ronald Reagan.[22] Even though he is married to celebrity Maria Shriver, daughter of Sargent Shriver and Eunice Kennedy, the macho actor has kept his conservative Republican beliefs. Bush political consultants felt that high visibility photo opportunities of the president with Arnold Schwarzenegger helped Bush keep a macho image, and it impressed many of the young apolitical male and female teenage fans that followed Schwarzenegger.[23]

Schwarzenegger became famous in pop culture terms in 1984 when he played the lead role in *Terminator*. He appeared as an indestructible, man-made, metal robot of a new technological master race. His job in the movie was to kill a woman, played by Linda Hamilton, who was going to have a baby who would become the leader of the human race in a post–nuclear war period in the future. In 1991, Schwarzenegger returned to play in *Terminator 2*, only this time he played a metal robot creature who changed sides in this future war to protect the heroic woman, again played by actress Linda Hamilton. There was speculation in 2001 that he would run as a Republican for governor in California.

MARTIN SHEEN

Another politically committed film and television star is Martin Sheen. Since 1986 Sheen has been particularly active in the movement to help the homeless. Sheen played homeless activist Mitch Snyder in a television movie called "Samaritan." He took his role to heart and began his own efforts to help the homeless. He helped build soup kitchens and raise money for the homeless throughout the late 1980s.

Sheen is best known as an outstanding peace activist. He opposes U.S. military production of nuclear arms. Sheen belongs to a group called American Peace Test that demonstrates against the testing of nuclear weapons. He has been arrested over thirty times since 1986 in peaceful, nonviolent sit-ins at nuclear test sites and at nuclear production facilities around the country. He now stars as president in the popular NBC television show, *West Wing*.

SYLVESTER STALLONE

Sometimes actors are forced into the role of being a celebrity politico because of the kinds of movie parts they play. Sylvester Stallone became a pop culture symbol in the 1980s because of his movie roles in *Rocky* and *Rambo*. Although his private, personal politics could be described as liberal, Stallone became a symbol for the conservative right-wing establishment because of the one-man efforts in the movies to fight injustice, Vietnamese soldiers, and the Soviet military. Each *Rambo* sequel had Stallone playing a more patriotic, militaristic, jingoistic, macho killer than the previous *Rambo* movie. "Rambo" became a word to describe Ronald Reagan's foreign policy, and it was a word used by opinion leaders to describe Reagan himself. Posters appeared with Ronald Reagan's head superimposed over Stallone's militant, muscular frame, and he was called "Ronbo." Conservative politicians courted Stallone in the 1980s so they could have their pictures taken with Rambo.

ROCK STARS

In the late 1960s and early 1970s, there were a few consistent rock politicos who showed a social conscience.[24] Folksingers like Arlo Guthrie, Phil Ochs, and Joan Baez played many social and political benefits to show that they really cared. Guthrie did political benefits to back Chilean freedom fighters. Ochs played the May Day Demonstrations of 1971 that proclaimed, "If the government won't stop the war (Vietnam), then we'll stop the government." Ochs also organized a tribute in 1974 for Salvador Allende, who had been assassinated during the military coup of 1973 in Chile, and Ochs played his last major rally that celebrated the end of the Vietnam War in 1975 before he committed suicide in 1976. Baez provided a model of a consistent social activist who played all the demonstrations, rallies, and even did the talk show circuit to promote progressive causes. Baez became "Saint Joan" to the antiwar movement and invested as much energy as anyone in the movement to end the war in Indochina.

In 1971, George Harrison performed a Concert for Bangladesh to raise money for the starving refugees in Bangladesh. He persuaded Bob Dylan, Ringo Starr, Billy Preston, and others to play the benefit at Madison Square Garden. The show raised about $240,000 for the United Nations Children's Fund for Relief to Refugee Children of Bangladesh, and it established the model of the rock benefit concert. Other concerts were performed in the 1970s for causes such as Bay Area charities, prison reform, the Cambodian refugees, the Vietnamese boat people, elimination of world hunger, and the fight to end racism.

Perhaps one of the most remarkable records of achievement by a politico pop star in the 1970s was the performance of singer-songwriter Harry Chapin. This musician played for many causes in the 1970s, but he was particularly concerned about world hunger. He became a full-fledged food activist and lobbyist on Capitol Hill as he appeared before congressional hearings and on congressional doorsteps. By 1978, Chapin and other activists put enough pressure on the appropriate power points in Washington to get Congress to call for the establishment of a Presidential Commission on Domestic and International Hunger and Malnutrition.[25] From 1973 to 1981, Chapin raised about $500,000 per year for world hunger, and he targeted the money for effective relief efforts. In 1977, Chapin had his friends John Denver, James Taylor, and Gordon Lightfoot join him in a concert to fight world hunger given in Detroit.

One of the most interesting uses of rock music for social change happened in 1979 with a series of rock concerts and one public rally in New York City sponsored by Musicians United for Safe Energy or MUSE. These "No Nukes" concerts were started by the organizers of MUSE to raise money and consciousness about the issue of nuclear energy. The idea for MUSE came from John Hall, Jackson Browne, Bonnie Raitt, and Graham Nash.[26] Hall wrote "Power," an anti–nuclear power song. The other rock stars in MUSE became alarmed about nuclear power when the proposed nuclear power plant at Diablo Canyon in California was pushed in the mid 1970s. Jackson Browne became politicized over this issue and donated the sale of T-shirts at his concerts to the anti–nuclear power movement, but the Madison Square Garden concerts moved into a new realm of political activism. The money raised by "No Nukes" was to be put into local anti–nuclear power groups around the country.

After the great success of the "No Nukes" concerts, Jackson Browne continued his political activism in the early 1980s. Browne became a strong supporter of the nuclear freeze movement to stop the arms race. In the summer of 1982, Browne, Linda Ronstadt, and James Taylor played benefit concerts in New York City for the nuclear freeze movement. In California, the anti–nuclear weapons freeze movement raised money in the summer of 1982 with a concert from Bob Dylan, Joan Baez, Stevie Wonder, Bette Midler, and others. In Denver, a nuclear freeze concert heard Jimmy Buffett, John Denver, and Judy Collins. This week of activity ended in Central Park in New York where 800,000 people marched against nuclear weapons. The 600,000 people who could jam into the park for the speeches and songs listened to various groups.

Browne turned his attention to the so-called secret war in Nicaragua. Over the 1980s, Browne became a consistent and persistent critic of Ronald Reagan's militaristic policy toward El Salvador and Nicaragua. He played concerts, donated money, wrote songs on his albums, and gave media interviews to combat Reagan's war against social change in Central America.

Stevie Wonder became a strong opponent of apartheid in South Africa, and he helped finally to win the struggle for a Martin Luther King, Jr., holiday because of his organizing, lobbying, musical, and celebrity political abilities.

The important turning point in the celebrity political system for rock stars came with the Live Aid concerts in 1985. Irish rocker Bob Geldof conceived of the international live rock concert to raise money for starving people in Ethiopia. Geldof had heard of all the rockers who made a record for Christmas, 1984, called Band Aid and Geldof knew of American efforts to raise consciousness in "We Are the World" recordings. Most importantly, Geldof had seen a BBC film of the suffering, starvation, and death due to the famine in Ethiopia and because of the political problems of food distribution. He organized two giant concerts on July 13, 1985, from Wembley Stadium in London and in Philadelphia called "Live Aid." The international television broadcast of the event reached over a billion people and, for the first time since global citizens watched men on the moon in 1969, the world was technologically united during the transmission. At least $140 million was raised for starving people in Ethiopia, but more importantly, for a few days, consciousness was raised over the issue.

For his efforts, Geldof was dubbed "Saint Bob" by his peers in the rock industry and given knighthood in England. He became the first rock star ever to be nominated for the Nobel Peace Prize, and he met with the U.S. Congress, the British Parliament, Prime Minister Margaret Thatcher, Mother Teresa, Queen Elizabeth, and other world leaders to discuss the problem of starvation in Ethiopia. He addressed the European Parliament, and he lectured the United Nations General Assembly on the problem of famine and food distribution.[27]

At Live Aid, Bob Dylan told the crowd that they should give some money to the American farmers instead of sending it all to Ethiopia. Willie Nelson, Neil Young, and John Cougar Mellencamp were impressed by Dylan's sentiments and organized "Farm Aid." Mellencamp even recorded songs on his *Scarecrow* and *Lonesome Jubilee* album about the plight of the American farmer. Willie Nelson and John Mellencamp also testified in support of the Family Farm Bill and told legislators that government needed to help bail out the ailing family farmers. Farm Aid did not solve the problems of the American family farmers who were being driven off their farms, but like Live Aid, the Farm Aid concerts raised some money and raised much national consciousness about the issue.

One singer in the 1980s who helped revive social consciousness in her art was singer-songwriter Tracy Chapman. This black folksinger made it fashionable to have an overt political message in one's songs once again. Chapman sang songs about the homeless, racism, spousal abuse, and even about the coming "revolution." Not only did Tracy Chapman sing with a social conscience, but also she performed a tribute to Nelson Mandela at Freedom Fest in September 1988, and she was a featured performer at Amnesty International concerts around the globe, including the Human Rights Now tour, along with Bruce Springsteen, Peter Gabriel, and Sting.[28]

Bruce Springsteen was a rock politico who became a cultural icon. The artist employed a quiet political activism by playing benefits for Vietnam veterans, unemployed mill workers, and the homeless. However, in 1988, Springsteen became more publicly political as he headlined the Amnesty International Human Rights Now tour along with Sting, Tracy Chapman, Peter Gabriel, and others. This was an enormously successful series of concerts around the globe that called worldwide attention to the problem of political prisoners and their treatment.[29]

A more radical form of political activism came from rap groups. Especially among young minority audiences, rap has proven to be very popular and sometimes political in its representation of the world faced by nonwhite teenagers.[30] Artists like MC Hammer and Vanilla Ice toned down the most strident messages of rap and made the art form more palatable to mainstream, white America. Rap music found its way into commercials, movie soundtracks, and, of course, music videos.

Yet it was the hard-core rap artists who provided the political fireworks among middle-class America. One group, Boogie Down Productions, led by KRS ONE preached a message of black cultural heritage, pride in education, and standing up for one's rights. KRS ONE (rapper Chris Parker) said his name stood for "Knowledge Reigns Supreme Over Nearly Everyone." He is a well-known and respected artist in the rap community with his hip social and political raps. He teaches that knowledge is crucial for maintaining African-American identity. His most political raps include "Who Protects Us?" "Love's Gonna Get You," and "You Must Learn." In "You Must Learn," he tells of the class situation that African Americans face in the United States.

Rap group Public Enemy scored big fame and fear among some white citizens with a rap "Fight the Power," and the most successful hard-core rap group was N.W.A. or "Niggarz With Attitude." N.W.A. talked about gang violence, sex, drugs, police, and racism. They used tough street profanities and their lyrics were very sexist. They rapped songs like "the Police" and "Dope Man." N.W.A. surprised everyone by releasing an album that was too hot, obscene, foul, and nasty to play on AM-FM radio. Nevertheless, the album "EFIL4ZRAGGIN" or backwards "Niggarz 4 Life" was shipped as the number-one record album in the country upon release because of very strong word-of-mouth promotion and notoriety.

It was these groups that attracted the ire of neoconservatives such as William Bennett and "New Democrats" such as Joe Lieberman. Concerned over what they regarded as the glorification of sex and violence, these men lobbied music company executives to clean up these lyrics and raise the moral standards presented to young Americans. In their view, rap lyrics were debasing the country's civic life and endangering the future of the United States.[31]

The issue even became the subject of candidate comments in the 2000 election. George W. Bush openly worried about declining values in America and pointed toward the entertainment and music industries as major culprits. "The freedom we cherish ultimately depends on the values our families cherish. We must give our children a spirit of moral courage," he said. Unless Hollywood cleaned up its act, he warned, more government intervention would be required.[32]

Not wanting to be outdone on this issue, Gore also emphasized the importance of family values. Similar to his wife Tipper, who had worked earlier to clean up album lyrics, Gore devoted part of his basic presentation to values. However, unlike Bush, he noted that families were a long-term American value, and therefore something to be highly respected. The government must work to see that entertainers respected basic community moral standards.[33]

Yet Bush claimed that Gore's rhetoric on values rang hollow. "At the beginning of the week, he sounded awfully tough on Hollywood," Bush recalled. "After a couple of fund-raisers, he's changing his tune. After going out there to Hollywood to collect some money, no longer is it six months and tough talk."[34]

CONCLUSION

To conclude, it is obvious that a wide range of television, movie, and musical performers have become involved in the political process. From making contributions to candidates and parties to lobbying public officials on behalf of particular causes, these celebrity activists attract press attention to various issues and explain why the public should be concerned. With the aid of willing media reporters, this kind of coverage affects the national political agenda and sometimes even the deliberation of congressional legislators. It is likely that issues such as violence against women, handgun regulation, and hunger would not have attracted as much press as they have without the assistance of prominent Hollywood entertainers. In this way, then, such individuals have become important to the manner in which the American political system functions.

NOTES

1. Robert Sheppard, "Trouble at the Megaplex," *Maclean's*, 22 January 2001.
2. Ronald Brownstein, *The Power and the Glitter* (New York: Pantheon, 1990), pp. 92–100.
3. Len Sherman, *The Good, the Bad, and the Famous* (New York: Lyle Stuart, 1990), p. 26.
4. Charlie Chaplin, *My Life in Pictures* (New York: Grosset & Dunlap, 1975).
5. Helen Gahagan Douglas, *A Full Life: Helen Gahagan Douglas* (Garden City, NY: Doubleday, 1982).
6. John Orman, "The Impact of Popular Music in Society: America's Musical Pulse," (Westport, CT: Greenwood Press, 1992).

7. Jim Rutenberg, "Some Star Presence amid Talking Heads," *New York Times*, 15 May 2000, p. C-20.
8. Jim Rutenberg, "Some Star Presence amid Talking Heads," *New York Times*, 15 May 2000, p. C-20.
9. See Carlo Fiore, *Bud: The Brando I Knew* (New York: Delacorte Press, 1974); Anna Kashfi Brando, *Brando for Breakfast* (New York: Crown Publishers, 1979); Charles Higham, *Brando: The Unauthorized Biography* (New York: New American Library, 1987); and Christopher Nickens, *Brando: A Biography in Pictures* (New York: Doubleday Press, 1987).
10. Jim Sullinger, "Snowbarger Campaign Gets Help from Heston," *Kansas City Star*, 30 October 1998, p. C-3.
11. Melinda Henneberger, "Rallying Voters and Relishing a Leading Role," *New York Times*, 3 November 2000, p. A-23.
12. Paul Witteman, "Go Ahead Voters, Make My Day," *Time*, April 1986, p. 30, and Pamela Leigh, "Not-so-Tough Talk from Clint Eastwood," *Ladies Home Journal*, June 1989, p. 38.
13. Fred L. Guiles, *Jane Fonda: The Actress in Her Time* (New York: Pinnacle Books, 1982), Chapter 28, and see Christopher Anderson, *Citizen Jane* (New York: Dell, 1991), Chapter 18.
14. Mitchell Fink and Lauren Rubin, "Jane Fonda Staging a Return to Acting," *New York Daily News*, 16 January 2001, p. 19.
15. Fred Shuster, "Streisand Sings Praises of Democrats," *Cleveland Plain Dealer*, 18 August 2000, p. 5-E.
16. Ed Henry, "Hello Senate!" *Roll Call*, 2 April 2001, p. 1.
17. *Irish Times*, "The Cult of Oprah," 5 August 2000, p. 61.
18. Lynn Sweet, "Bush, Gore in Hot Seat with Oprah," *Chicago Sun-Times*, 10 September 2000, p. A-23.
19. Maria LaGanga, "The Softer Side of Bush," *Los Angeles Times*, 20 September 2000, p. A-15.
20. Lynn Sweet, "Bush, Gore in Hot Seat with Oprah," *Chicago Sun-Times*, 10 September 2000, p. A-23.
21. William Booth, "Pundits Go Batty for Beatty," *Washington Post*, 31 August 1999.
22. Dan Geringer, "As They Say in Hollywood . . . Pex Sell Tix," *Sports Illustrated*, 7 December 1987, pp. 82–90 and Craig Neff, "Twist a Few Arms, Conan," *Sports Illustrated*, 14 May 1990, p. 114.
23. Ronald Brownstein, *The Power and the Glitter*, p. 377.
24. John Orman, *The Politics of Rock Music* (Chicago: Nelson-Hall, 1984).
25. Dave Marsh, "Singing for the World's Supper," *Rolling Stone*, 6 April 1978, p. 32.
26. Daisann McLane, "MUSE: Rock Politics Comes of Age," *Rolling Stone*, 15 November 1978, p. 10. See also John Rockwell, "Rock Stars Are into Politics Again," *New York Times*, 16 September 1979, Arts and Leisure section, p. 22 and Debra Rae Cohen, "John Hall: Power Is the Only Issue," *Rolling Stone*, 23 August 1979, pp. 18–19.
27. Robert Geldof, *Is That It? The Autobiography* (New York and London: Weidenfeld and Nicholson, 1986). See also Robin Denselow, *When the Music's Over* (Boston and London: Faber and Faber, 1989), pp. 244–249.
28. Richard Stengel, "Singing for Herself," *Time*, 12 March 1990, pp. 70–71 and Sheila Rogers, "10,000 Maniacs and Tracy Chapman," *Rolling Stone*, 16 June 1988, p. 38.

29. Kurt Loder, "Bruce Springsteen," *Rolling Stone*, 6 December 1984, pp. 18–22; Dave Marsh, *Born to Run* (New York: Pantheon, 1987); and Charles Cross, *Backstreets* (New York: Harmony, 1989).

30. Chuck D., *Fight the Power: Rap, Race, and Reality* (New York: Delacorte Press, 1997) and Ronin Ro, *Gangsta: Merchandizing the Rhymes of Violence* (New York: St. Martin's Press, 1996).

31. Richard Harrington, "Guilty: Free Speech in the First Degree," *Washington Post*, 9 June 1996, p. G-4 and William J. Bennett, *The Book of Virtues: A Treasury of Great Moral Stories* (New York: Simon & Schuster, 1993).

32. Robert Jackson, "Bush Asks Christian Coalition for Support," *Los Angeles Times*, 1 October 2000, p. A-23.

33. *Houston Chronicle*, "Bush, Gore Take Hard Aim at the Middle," 13 October 2000, p. A-40.

34. Maria LaGanga, "Bush Portrays Gore as Hypocrite on Hollywood Issue," *Los Angeles Times*, 21 September 2000, p. A-19.

Sports Politicos

If organized religion is the opiate of the masses, as Karl Marx maintained, then perhaps the organized sports system in the United States is the opiate for Americans. The entertaining sports system dominates American television, news coverage, and social life. A disproportionate amount of space in newspapers is given to sports coverage, and sports coverage dominates hallway conversations. Many citizens follow sports to such a degree that they are removed from serious political thought about crisis issues facing the United States. Richard Lipsky has noted that the United States resembles a "jockocracy" in that sports talk dominates the political and business worlds for Americans.[1]

Sports entertainers are among the highest paid celebrities in the United States. The boxer Evander Holyfield tallied about $60 million for his fighting skills and Mike Tyson earned about $30 million at his peak. Between golf victories and commercial endorsements, Tiger Woods makes around $54 million a year, much of it in endorsements for the twelve different companies he works with.[2]

When he was starring for the Chicago Bulls basketball team, Michael Jordan earned up to $50 million a year between basketball and endorsements. Ever since Kirby Puckett became the first $3-million-a-year professional baseball player in 1989, baseball salaries have escalated rapidly. Texas Ranger Alex Rodriguez is under contract for $252 million over a ten-year period. Derek Jeter of the New York Yankees is being paid $189 million over ten years. Boston Red Sox player Manny Ramirez earns $160 million over an eight year period.[3] Top basketball star Shaquille O'Neal of the Los Angeles Lakers inked a contact that pays him $26.5 million in 2003, $29.4 million in 2004, and $32.4 million in 2005, which makes him the highest-paid athlete (on a per-year basis) in professional team sports.[4]

In the celebrity political system, politicians, and especially the American president, love to associate with sports heroes. The hope is that the glamour of the sports celebrity will rub off on the politician. The president only likes to have winners around him in order to project the image of a vigorous, winning president. Richard Nixon and George Bush liked to invite important NFL players to the White House, and Bush enjoyed calling up national champions after they had won the deciding contest on national television. The president gets to intrude on the public space of the winning team, and he gets a free association with the super sports champions. Ford not only liked to associate with professional sports champions, but also liked to participate in sports. Carter continued the trend with his love of sports heroes, tennis, softball, stock car racing, and running. Carter tried to bask in the glow of the U.S. Olympic Hockey team's Gold Medal in 1980 and for some analysts the miraculous victory of the amateur hockey team over the Soviet Union was one of the highlights of Carter's foreign policy.

It was Ronald Reagan who institutionalized the relationship between the White House and championship sports teams. Reagan systematically invited professional and collegiate champions to the White House for photo opportunities and television news feeds.[5] Reagan, who had been a sports announcer in the 1930s, loved joking with sports heroes. He would throw a baseball and shoot the puck at a goalie. He would work out on an exercise machine and throw football. All of these moves would make national news to show that the president was the nation's top sports fan. In 1988, Reagan even did play-by-play for one and one-half innings for the Chicago Cubs along with the legendary broadcaster Harry Caray. News network CNN covered the president live while he called the game. Reagan even called off his inaugural parade and ceremonies for January 20, 1985, because they conflicted with the NFL Super Bowl festivities.

Bush continued Reagan's role as the top sports fan by inviting championship teams to the White House. Bush not only celebrated sports winners, but also competed in more sporting activities than any other American president in history. Bush competed in or tried at least two dozen sports when he became president. He enjoyed being photographed with sports celebrities and to perhaps shoot a basketball for the cameras. After he left the presidency, Bush became the oldest former chief executive to go parachute-jumping. One sports celebrity, Michael Jordan of the NBA Championship Chicago Bulls, was harshly criticized for boycotting the White House ceremonies with President Bush, thereby becoming the first sports celebrity to refuse to let the president of the United States cash in on his celebrityhood.

President Clinton spent considerable time watching sports on television (especially teams associated with his home state, the University of Arkansas Razorbacks), and continued the practice of inviting winning championship teams to the White House for a photo opportunity. It gave him a chance to bask in the glow of the winner and an opportunity to be photographed around young people. Cognizant of his personal weight problem, Clinton went jogging on a regular basis, although he also invited the ridicule of satirists when he sometimes would stop at McDonalds on the way home from the run.[6]

George W. Bush allocated two hours a day for personal exercise. His major activity was running, where he ran three miles a day at a pace of seven minutes and fifteen seconds a mile. But he also enjoyed hunting and fishing when he returned to his native Texas. Similar to his father, Bush plays golf. Striking a clear contrast with Clinton who had a reputation for retaking shots that didn't turn out well, his golfing partners pointed out that Bush takes "no mulligans. . . . He's a stickler for rules. He'll play the ball where it lies."[7]

Bush was the first owner of a major league sports franchise (the Texas Rangers) to hold the office of the presidency. During his time operating the Rangers, Bush appeared at most home games sitting in field boxes with the fans, not the owner's box. He led the fight for the city of Arlington, Texas, to build the team a new stadium, and made $19 million when he sold his interest in the team. He lived and breathed the sports culture, and regularly inserted sports metaphors into his public remarks. Among his prize personal possessions was a collection of 250 autographed balls that he showcased in his Texas governor's office. His favorite item in the group was a ball that had been autographed by baseball legends Joe DiMaggio and Ted Williams.[8]

With the close integration of sports and politics, it is no surprise that sports figures have come to play a major role in American politics. Not only do sports celebrities endorse presidential candidates, raise money, and allow themselves to be used by politicians, but also sports celebrities sometimes cross over into the political arena and become famed nonpoliticos who run for office. A number of celebrity sports heroes have been elected as major governmental officeholders.

Sports politicos so far have been almost all male. However, the passage of Title IX and the resulting encouragement of women's athletes suggests that in future years there may emerge greater gender diversity in the system of sports celebrityhood.

As demonstrated in the profiles on the following pages, men such as Bill Bradley (senator from New Jersey), Jim Bunning (senator from Kentucky), Jack Kemp (House of Representatives, New York), Jesse Ventura (governor of Minnesota), and Jim Ryun, Steve Largent, and J. C. Watts (House of Representatives) have achieved great political success. Unlike many Hollywood entertainers, who tend to lean left in their political views, many former athletes have run as conservative Republicans who are opposed to high taxes and big government.

ATHLETES TURNED POLITICIANS

BILL BRADLEY

In 1977, Bill Bradley retired from professional basketball after a legendary career. Born and raised in Crystal City, Missouri, he had been one of the best high school basketball players in the United States from 1958 to 1961. Bradley went on to become an All-American basketball player at Princeton University. He played on the 1964 Olympic Gold Medal–winning basketball team and, in his senior year at Princeton, he led the Tigers to the Final Four where he scored fifty-eight points in the consolation game to break Oscar Robertson's scoring record. Bradley was a brilliant student and serious academic. After Princeton, he received a Rhodes Scholarship to attend Oxford. After Oxford, "Dollar Bill" Bradley joined the New York Knicks and started a glorious professional basketball career that lasted ten years. He was part of the storied New York Knicks basketball team that won the NBA Championship in 1970 and 1973.

In 1978, Bradley announced that he would seek the U.S. Senate seat from New Jersey as a Democratic candidate. Movie stars, baseball players, football players, POWs, generals, astronauts, and other celebrities had been elected to public office by virtue of their name recognition, financial resources, media coverage, and celebrity; so Bradley figured, why not an intelligent basketball player? The voters from New Jersey agreed and Bradley was elected to his first term in 1978 and reelected in 1984 and 1990.

Bradley worked on tax reform and became known as a Democrat who concentrated on fiscal issues. He was labeled as a boring stump speaker, but he attracted large audiences virtually everywhere he went. Everyone wanted to see the great Bill Bradley. But as with most everything else Bradley had done in his life, he began to grow and develop as a public servant. He became a major player on the tax-reform issue and, after he was reelected in 1984, he began a national push to make the tax code fairer and simpler. By 1986 Bradley helped push through the Tax Reform Act, and his name began to be dropped by national columnists as a likely presidential candidate for the Democrats. Initially, Bradley rejected the pleas from some of his followers and decided not to run for the presidency or to seek the vice-presidential nomination in 1988. His growth as a national politician was unfinished.

In the early 1990s, Bradley's national fame and recognition as a talented, caring, concerned, pragmatic, serious national leader was well developed, yet he refused to run for the American presidency because he didn't think he was ready yet to serve as American president. He had many more national issues that he wanted to read up on.[9] Bradley became a strong voice in the U.S. Senate in fighting racism, sexism, and in working for family issues like day care, Head Start, education, and health care. He became an environmental activist and a national senator who displayed clear compassion to the downtrodden.

It was not until 2000 that Bradley decided to run for the Democratic nomination for president against Al Gore. Initially, his prospects looked good. Surprising the experts, who gave him little chance, Bradley raised almost as much money as did the sitting vice president. In fall of 1999, Bradley attracted extensive news coverage from the media and in some polls in early primary states in the Northeast, pulled virtually even with Gore.[10]

Although Bradley succeeded in raising some novel approaches to health care and education, in the end this nonpolitician was beaten by a professional politician. With the skill of a precision boxer, Gore picked apart Bradley's reform proposals and made his challenger look too liberal for the national mainstream. Gore beat Bradley in Iowa and New Hampshire and coasted to victory in the remaining states.

However, Bradley scored one notable achievement in the era of celebrity politics. He attracted great attention when he won celebrity endorsements from Michael Jordan of the Bulls and Bill Russell of the Boston Celtics. Both sports stars appeared in ads for Bradley and gave a short-term boost to Bradley's lagging campaign. In the end, though, Jordan's first foray into national politics was not enough to propel Bradley to the Democratic presidential nomination.

JIM BUNNING

Jim Bunning won election to the U.S. Senate from Kentucky in 1998. He had been a Hall of Fame pitcher for the Detroit Tigers and Philadelphia Phillies. At the time of his retirement in 1971, he ranked number two on the list of number of strikeouts, falling behind only the legendary pitcher Walter Johnson.

Unlike the usual pattern of celebrity politicians, Bunning had worked his way up the political ladder over a period of two decades. After his retirement from baseball, he ran for a city council seat in 1977, was elected to the Kentucky Senate in 1979, and won a U.S. House seat in 1986. In that body, he served on the Ways and Means Committee and chaired the Social Security subcommittee.[11]

His U.S. Senate race was a hard-fought campaign in which Bunning sought to move more to the political center. In his House races, he had ran as a conservative Republican who would be tough on abortion rights and flag-burning. However, by 1998, Bunning repositioned himself as a defender of Social Security, health care, and education. In his 1998 campaign, Bunning broadcast negative attacks on his opponent. The strategy led his opponent Scott Baesler (a former basketball star at the University of Kentucky) to comment that Bunning "always [has] been a little strident. In his playing days, I guess, you knocked the other guy down with a baseball if you didn't like him."[12] In one of the closest contests that year, Bunning beat Baesler by a razor-thin margin.

JACK KEMP

Jack Kemp was a professional football quarterback for the Buffalo Bills. In his thirteen-year career, he led the Bills to back-to-back American Football League championships in 1964 and 1965. In 1965 he was named as the Most Valuable Player in the league. He was cofounder of the AFL Player's Association, and was elected president of the group.

After retiring from football, Kemp decided to seek a seat in the U.S. House of Representatives to represent the citizens of Buffalo, New York. Kemp won the seat in 1971 and served until 1989 as the respected, conservative congressman from New York.

While Kemp was a member of the House of Representatives, he quickly became one of the Republican leaders in the House Republican Conference. In the late 1970s, he became a strong proponent of supply-side economics, and by the early 1980s, he had become one of the builders of Ronald Reagan's economic policies known as "Reaganomics." He authored the famous Kemp-Roth tax cut for 1981–1983 that saw income taxes cut and revenues shrink by 10 percent in the first year, 10 percent in the second year and 5 percent in the third year. He felt Americans were overtaxed and that there was just too much big government. He thought that tax cuts would jump start the economy by allowing citizens to invest monies that would provide for jobs and economic growth. Moreover, he wasn't worried that the lack of revenues coming into the federal treasury might cause huge deficits, blaming the deficit problem on runaway government spending.

In 1988, Kemp ran for the U.S. presidency and some political writers thought he had an excellent chance to get the nomination in a wide open field of Republican candidates who lined up to carry on the Reagan legacy. Kemp's campaign failed to catch on in New Hampshire, but it did excite young conservatives aged eighteen to twenty-four years old.

In 1989, Kemp was appointed by President Bush to be the Secretary of the U.S. Department of Housing and Urban Development to restore confidence to a tattered cabinet position. During his time as HUD secretary, he revived a department that had been rocked by scandal. Kemp pushed for the Republican party to take the lead in providing the cities with a strategy of hope and growth. He wanted Republicans to deal with race relations, establish "enterprise zones," and build homes for the homeless. He was silenced by the Bush administration from 1989 to 1991 for the most part, but after the riots in Los Angeles following the acquittal of the police officers who beat Rodney King, Kemp suddenly looked like the future of the Republican party.

In 1996, he was nominated to run as the GOP candidate for vice president under Dole against Clinton and Gore. It was a surprise nomination because Kemp and Dole long had held different views on fiscal policy and tax cuts. But with Dole's campaign lagging, his advisors convinced the Kansas man to spice up his ticket with the celebrity vice presidential nominee. Dole initially earned positive news coverage for the pick, but the Dole-Kemp ticket still was beaten by Clinton-Gore.[13]

JIM RYUN

Jim Ryun was elected to the U.S. House of Representatives in 1996. A former 1968 Olympian who set a world record of 3:51:1 for running the mile at the University of Kansas, Ryun won an open-seat election. A spokesman for his Democrat opponent recognized the impact of having a celebrity name in the race. "Everyone who was around when Jim was competing was a fan," he pointed out.[18] Like most famed nonpoliticos, Ryun had no political experience prior to this run. Since his graduation from the University of Kansas, he had worked as an author and motivational speaker.[19]

Ryun was conservative in his politics, pro-military and pro-life, and in favor of cutting taxes and promoting family values. He made no secret of his Christian fundamentalist political beliefs. However, since he represented the rural area around Topeka, his views were consistent with majority sentiments within the congressional district. Since his first run, Ryun has been elected to the House several times.

J. C. WATTS

Julius Caesar Watts became the first black Republican elected in 1994 to the House of Representatives from a Southern state since Reconstruction. A former star quarterback at the University of Oklahoma, Watts led his team to the Orange Bowl in 1980 and 1981. Although originally a Democrat, Watts switched parties in 1989 and won statewide office in 1990 as head of the Oklahoma Corporation Commission.

After four years in that position, Watts sought and won the U.S. House seat. A conservative, Watts ran as a Republican in a district that was only 5 percent black because, as he stated, "Government needs to play a lesser role in people's lives. I am a believer that over the past forty years government has been more of a hindrance than a help to the minority community." Throughout the campaign, Watts criticized President Clinton for allowing gays in the military and being a proponent of abortion rights. "I don't think we should measure compassion by how many people are on food stamps and public housing. I think we should measure compassion by how few people we have on food stamps and public housing," Watts proclaimed.[20]

Watts went on to hold a high-ranking position among House Republicans. He is chairman of the House Republican Conference, a ranking position within the leadership, and he has given hundreds of speeches across the country on behalf of Republican candidates. His conservative rhetoric attracted criticism from other black leaders, such as Jesse Jackson, Jr. Speaking of black Republicans, Jackson noted that many of them have "positioned themselves against black needs to gain white applause."[21]

When asked why he was conservative given the fact that most blacks are liberal Democrats, Watts explained that many black athletes are more conservative because of the high taxes they pay off their large sports salaries. "When you make a lot of dollars, people should want to protect their interests," he said. "Athletes have been good at giving back, but you can't unload a wagon from an empty wagon."[22]

STEVE LARGENT

Steve Largent had been a pass receiver for the Seattle Seahawks for fourteen years before his sports retirement in 1989. In honor of his accomplishments, he was elected to the National Football League Hall of Fame in 1995. He attended Tulsa University in the 1970s.[23] Largent was elected to the House of Representatives in 1994. Winning a six-way Republican primary that year, Largent went into the House and has been reelected ever since.

During his first run for Congress, opponents attacked him as a carpetbagger, a charge that is common with famed nonpoliticos. Noting that he had spent most of his time in the state of Washington, one Republican complained, "Why doesn't he run out of Seattle? He was up there for fourteen years, a lot longer than he's been here [in Tulsa]."[24] The comment, though, did not prevent Largent from winning the primary.

A fundamentalist Christian, Largent is conservative on social and fiscal policy. He is a member of the House Commerce Committee, where he serves on the energy and power subcommittee. Largent opposed many Clinton initiatives during the 1990s and staked out political positions that were in line with his Tulsa congressional district.

ATHLETES AS POLITICAL ACTIVISTS

MAGIC JOHNSON

In 1991, the sports world was shocked to learn that basketball legend Earvin "Magic" Johnson, the definitive point guard for the Los Angeles Lakers, was retiring from the National Basketball Association because he was HIV positive. The network news divisions covered the story almost with the same intensity as a presidential assassination attempt.

Magic Johnson was a superstar celebrity basketball player known for his college heroics at Michigan State in 1979 to win the NCAA basketball championship and for his many professional NBA championships with the Los Angeles Lakers during the 1980s. His marquee matchups with Larry Bird of the Boston Celtics helped the NBA gain a wide television audience. Johnson was also known for his many endorsements of commercial products. He was perhaps one of the most beloved professional athletes competing in the 1990s, and suddenly he was forced to retire to protect his health. It was a shocking development for many of his fans.

Johnson quickly became the major celebrity spokesperson for the HIV-positive and AIDS epidemic in the United States. He appeared on the "Arsenio Hall" show and talked about how to have safe sex. He gave interviews and taped specials for children about AIDS. He was named by President Bush to be a member of the National Commission on AIDs, and he took his role seriously.

At a giant media event staged by Bush to show that he cared about Magic Johnson and thus AIDS victims, Johnson stole the show. He urged President Bush to get into the "game" and try to stop AIDS with more government funding for research. He asked the president to become personally involved in the fight against AIDS because Johnson felt Bush had not "been there" in the struggle.[14]

Later, in 1992, Johnson continued his high-visibility role as celebrity spokesperson against AIDS. He was joined by talented tennis champion Arthur Ashe who had also unfortunately contracted the AIDS virus. Ashe had been informed by the USA Today sports department that the paper had a source who claimed Ashe had the AIDS virus. Rather than allow the media to release the story, Ashe held a press conference and announced that he had contracted the virus through a blood transfusion during a heart operation. He felt that the media had "outed" him and he became a reluctant spokesperson against AIDS in his own quiet way.

Magic Johnson, on the other hand, remains an outspoken champion of AIDS causes. He is also a prominent role model for others who may be HIV-positive, proving that not only can HIV-positive individuals survive, but also they can be highly successful. Johnson eventually built a $500 million empire featuring movie cinemas, T.G.I. Fridays restaurants, and Starbucks coffee shops, all built in inner-city locales. In 2001, Johnson was being touted as a possible congressional candidate for Democrats.[15]

MUHAMMAD ALI

Boxer Muhammad Ali became a strong sports politico because of his religious beliefs, which challenged the political system. In 1960 as a kid from Louisville, Kentucky, Cassius Clay won the Gold Medal for Olympic boxing. When he returned to Louisville, he found out he was still not allowed to eat in all-white restaurants in the segregated city. He went on to win the heavyweight boxing championship of the world by defeating Sonny Liston. He soon became a Muslim and followed the teachings of Elijah Muhammad. Clay changed his name to Muhammad Ali and demanded that sports writers call him by his new Muslim name. He continued to win fights and established himself as one of the greatest boxers in history.

However, the war in Vietnam changed Ali's life like it changed that of so many other Americans. Ali tried to get a conscientious objector draft classification because his Muslim religion did not allow him to kill another human being in the name of the state. He would only follow God's teachings, and besides, he did not think it was morally correct for white people to send black people to kill Asian people. His draft board refused to allow him a CO classification and quickly classified him as 1-A, or most likely to be drafted. Soon Ali was drafted into the U.S. military and refused to be inducted. He was indicted for refusing to fight and the powers of the boxing world stripped Ali of his boxing title, something that he never would have lost in the fight ring at that time since he clearly was at the top of his sport.

Ali became a spokesperson for African Americans in the black power movement, and because of his political activities and his principled stand he became a hero to many young whites in the antiwar movement. Later, in the late 1960s, the Supreme Court would throw out Ali's indictment because he was denied due process. This cleared the way for Ali to reenter the fight world, and he soon regained his heavyweight boxing championship.

In the 1970s, Ali was probably the most recognizable American citizen in the so-called Third World. He was a sports superstar of global scale. President Jimmy Carter even sent Ali to various African nations as his ambassador of goodwill when Carter wanted to sell African nations on some of his foreign policy ideas.[16] Ali became such a celebrity that in 2000 he was named to light the Olympic torch at its internationally broadcast opening ceremonies.[17]

OTHER SPORTS POLITICOS

The organized sports world contains many other athletes and coaches who often cross over into the political arena because their celebrity status allows them a forum to express their political views. Former Cleveland Browns fullback Jim Brown became a strong voice for black rights in the 1960s and 1970s. Superstars like Boston Celtics center Bill Russell and Atlanta Braves home-run hitter Henry Aaron became activists for civil rights and the rights of athletes while they played and after they retired. Kareem Abdul-Jabbar spoke out against the war in Vietnam when he played center for UCLA in the 1960s as Lew Alcindor. Later, after changing his name, Abdul-Jabbar became a major voice for black rights from the sports world when he played professional basketball for the Milwaukee Bucks and Los Angeles Lakers.

Another UCLA center, Bill Walton, not only spoke out against the war in Vietnam during the early 1970s, but also attacked President Nixon for his leadership, and attacked the FBI for violations of civil liberties.[25] In 1968, two sprinters, John Carlos and Tommy Smith, became noted political activists when they gave the black power fist salute while receiving medals during the 1968 Olympics in Mexico City.[26] Finally, another basketball player, Tom McMillan, was elected to the House of Representatives from Maryland in the

1980s, and he quickly started investigating the status of college athletics in terms of educational corruption, NCAA administration, and the shame of college athletics.

CONCLUSION

In short, it is clear that sports celebrities have become a major growth industry in the American political system. Once a relatively rare phenomena, it no longer is uncommon for star athletes to use their high name identification and financial resources to gain a seat in the House or Senate. There now are around a dozen former athletes who serve in the U.S. Congress, a number that is up over previous decades.

Athletes share many of the same kinds of advantages held by entertainment celebrities. Like their Hollywood brothers and sisters, sports stars do well in elections because of their high name identification, financial resources, favorable media coverage, and celebrity status in a society that values sports figures. Although athletes are not guaranteed political victory, their track record at running and winning elective office is generally positive, at least among male sports stars.

The one trend among athletes that is strikingly different from Hollywood entertainers is the relative conservatism of many former sports celebrities. Unlike Hollywood figures, who generally lean toward the liberal side of the political spectrum, former athletes often are more conservative in their political thinking. A number of the sports figures recently elected to the House, for example, have been Republicans.

When asked why this was the case, Bill Kenney, a former quarterback for the Kansas City Chiefs noted the party's emphasis on personal responsibility. "I believe the Republican philosophy is empowering individuals, helping individuals accomplish what they want to accomplish," he said. "Pro athletes realize they have to do it themselves."[27] These sports stars also are sensitive to tax issues owing to the fact that many of them made large amounts of money in a short period of time, thereby putting them in the highest tax bracket. With these kinds of concerns, it is logical for these individuals to run as Republican candidates.

NOTES

1. Richard Lipsky, *How We Play the Game* (Boston: Beacon Press, 1981).
2. Brian Trippe, "Disgruntled Woods Might Leave PGA," Dateline Alabama Web site, www.datelinealabama.com, November 14, 2000.
3. Buster Olney, "For Jeter, Being Part of Yanks' History Is Priceless," *New York Times*, 10 February 2001, p. B-15.

4. Broderick Turner, "Shaq to the Max," *Riverside Press-Enterprise*, 14 October 2000, p. C-1.
5. Ken Duberstein, "Rose Garden Ritual: Athletes on Parade," *New York Times*, 9 April 1989, p. 10-S.
6. Robert Russo and Philip Delves Broughton, "Mr. Bush Goes to Washington," *Ottawa Citizen*, 14 December 2000, p. A-3.
7. Ann Oldenburg, "The Bushes: Cut Out for Down-Home Fun," *USA Today*, 19 January 2001, p. 1-E.
8. Ann Oldenburg, "The Bushes: Cut Out for Down-Home Fun," *USA Today*, 19 January 2001, p. 1-E.
9. Gerri Hirshey, "Bradley's Time," *Rolling Stone*, 14 June 1990, pp. 57–70, 144.
10. Michael Kranish, "Poll Talk: Early Bradley Effort Touted," *Boston Globe*, 6 September 1999, p. A-1.
11. Information from Bunning's Web site at http://bunning.senate.gov.
12. R. W. Apple, Jr., "Fierce Opponents Go Down to the Wire," *New York Times*, 29 October 1998, p. A-26.
13. George Will, "Kemp Pick Lifts Republican Spirits," *Baltimore Sun*, 15 August 1996, p. 19-A.
14. Sherry Jackson, "Magic Urges Bush to Get into AIDS Game," *USA Today*, 15 January 1992, p. 1-A.
15. John Mercurio, "Magic's Slam-Dunk?: Johnson among Many Names Being Bounced around for Dixon Seat," *Roll Call*, 14 December 2000.
16. James Combs, *POLPOP* (Bowling Green, OH: Bowling Green University Popular Press, 1984), p. 66.
17. *Jakarta Post*, "The Sydney 2000 Olympics," 26 September 2000.
18. Robin Toner, "A Runner Runs for Congress," *New York Times*, 2 June 1996, p. 20.
19. Guy Gugliotta and John Yang, "Jim Ryun's Run Brings More Kick to Kansas Races," *Washington Post*, 2 June 1996, p. A-19.
20. Peter Brown, "Black Republican Hopes to Break Another Barrier," *Rocky Mountain News*, 24 October 1994, p. 26-A.
21. Kevin Merida, "Black Stars Rising in GOP," *Washington Post*, 30 October 1994, p. A-1.
22. Chris Dufresne, "Republicans Ride Sports Connection," *Los Angeles Times*, 15 August 2000, p. D-8.
23. Information from Largent Web site at www.house.gov.
24. Erik Brady, Debbie Becker, and Bob Abramson, "Largent Catches Some Flak," *USA Today*, 28 July 1994, p. 2-C.
25. Jack Scott, *The Athletic Revolution* (New York: Free Press, 1971). This was a book that influenced Bill Walton greatly.
26. David B. Kanin, *A Political History of the Olympic Games* (Boulder, CO: Westview Press, 1981), p. 94.
27. Steve Kraske, "Why Athletes Turn to GOP for a Career," *Kansas City Star*, 2 March 1998, p. A-2.

SATIRE: THE DOWNSIDE
OF CELEBRITYHOOD

From the beginning of the Republic, American humorists, satirists, and political cartoonists have pointed out the foibles of celebrity politicians and leaders. Indeed, one of the most serious drawbacks of being a celebrity is becoming the object of ridicule from humorists who love to attack prominent personalities. Famous people are easy to make fun of, owing to their general prominence, and their celebrity status often creates envy and resentment that encourages others to pick on their idiosyncrasies.

This pattern is not a recent phenomenon. As Bruce Granger has observed, "This conviction, that the satirist should attack vice and promote virtue, was voiced no less insistently in Revolutionary America than in Augustan, England."[1] Satirists lampooned the King, the Stamp Act, the British Parliament, and British law and customs at the outset. Ultimately, the King was overthrown, and humorists turned to homegrown figures.

Our early founders were not immune to satirical attacks on their policies, preferences, and personal behaviors. For example, George Washington was satirized as a "would-be" king whose autocratic methods should be feared. Alexander Hamilton was thought to favor a renewed union with England. Thomas Jefferson was criticized for having sex with one of his slaves, a charge that recently was documented using genetic evidence.[2]

In the nineteenth century, political cartoonists played an important role in pointing out the deficiencies of established democratic leaders as they helped shape opinion with respect to abolition, Tammany Hall, and the Civil War, for example. Mark Twain delighted in detailing the faults of politicians as well as his fellow men. For instance, in one of his writings, he noted that "barring that natural expression of villainy which we all have, the man looked honest enough." Referring to one of his fellow citizens, Twain commented that the individual was "an experienced, industrious, ambitious, and often quite picturesque liar."[3]

In the twentieth century, the political humor and satire of Will Rogers set a fine example of bipartisanship. Rogers went after Democrats and Republicans alike in his efforts to show the vices of the powerful and the problems of the high and mighty politician. A sampling of Rogers' insights from the 1920s and 1930s shows that the American distrust of political power and politicians runs deep. Will Rogers observed that "history has tried hard to teach us that we can't have good government under politicians. Now, to go and stick one at the very head of the government couldn't be wise."[4]

In the 1950s, one of our most colorful and provocative political satirists was Lenny Bruce. Bruce changed standup comedy forever as he challenged American society, Eisenhower and Nixon, racism, censorship, organized religion, patriotism, and authority. In this regard, he was one of the forerunners of antiestablishment comedians who became quite popular over the past several decades. There were no sacred cows in the eyes of Lenny Bruce. All establishment figures took it on the chin and sometimes between the eyes.

In his humorous routines, Bruce changed from a mainstream, Catskills funnyman to a political prophet.[5] In the early 1960s, Bruce increased the level of political intensity in his routines as he talked about Vietnam, the Kennedy assassination, political repression, the drug culture, and the civil rights movement. It was not long after that when authorities selected Lenny Bruce for prosecution with respect to his foul and abusive language.

When Bruce died of a drug overdose, the legacy of the hip, truth-telling comedian was passed on to Dick Gregory. Gregory's outstanding political routines of the late 1960s and early 1970s earned him a spot on Richard Nixon's enemies list. Gregory began to be politically active by doing benefits and marching with the civil rights movement as led by Dr. Martin Luther King, Jr. After King was assassinated in 1968, Gregory became a supreme political activist. He did concerts and benefits to end racism, to stop the war in Vietnam, to stop repression, and to aid the American Indian Movement. He raised money for the Black Panther party, and he appeared at the major peace rallies of the day. He was more of a social preacher and critic than a standup jokester. His routines were more like humorous political indictments of the values of the American political system. Gregory retired from active standup comedy entertaining in the 1970s to devote himself full-time to political activism.

The major forces for political humor and satire of American politics during that period came from *National Lampoon* magazine and the creative staff at the NBC television show *Saturday Night Live*. *National Lampoon* put out a devastating comedy album called *The Missing White House Tapes* in 1973, which cut, spliced, and edited Richard Nixon's statements about Watergate to simulate the truth. As events unfolded, *National Lampoon's* comedy "truth" began to closely resemble real events as they unfolded.

The comedy team on the innovative *Saturday Night Live* became important political humorists and satirists over several decades. Dan Akyroyd starred in skits that showed a "mean and scheming" Richard Nixon. Comedian Chevy Chase became a household word because of his Gerald Ford imitations. Chase played Ford as a dumb, bozo, jock president who had jello for brains.[6] His Ford-like pratfalls and physical-comedy portrayal of President Ford began what became known as Ford's "ridicule problem."

Political cartoonists like Gary Trudeau in "Doonesbury" also made Ford look like an absolute idiot. By making fun of Ford's stumbles and missteps, Trudeau painted the portrait of a man who was not on top of his job. The theme was picked up by other political cartoonists, and the national news media reinforced the idea that Ford was a dolt.

Sometimes within the first two or three stories of the evening, ABC, NBC, and CBS showed Ford making big gaffes and stupid sporting mistakes. Ford, who probably was one of the more athletic and graceful American presidents in the sporting world, was seen hitting his doubles partner in the back of the head with his serve in a tennis game. He was shown slicing a drive to hit a golf fan during a pro-am tournament. He was shown falling down at the bottom of a ski run and tripping at the foot of airplane ramps. He was shown confusing the states of Iowa with Ohio, and Israeli leader Menachem Begin with Egyptian President Anwar Sadat.

It was not long before the media began to run video to emphasize the image of Ford as national clown. Stand-up comedians ridiculed Ford as Ford jokes swept the country. Ford had played football too long at the University of Michigan without a helmet, it was joked, and national news showed Ford hitting his head getting out of a helicopter and falling down stairs as he exited his airplane.

The "ridicule problem" reached such epidemic proportions that Ford's White House staff advised the president to introduce *Saturday Night Live* and to let press secretary Ron Nessen be guest host of the show to indicate that the President could laugh at himself. Ford demonstrated he had a sense of humor by going along with the *Saturday Night Live* high jinks and Chevy Chase pratfalls. But many citizens saw Ford's participation and the collusion of his press secretary as absolute proof that Ford was a world class idiot.[7] In the close 1976 election with Jimmy Carter, Ford's "ridicule problem" was one of the factors that helped turn the tide against Ford's presidency. Among the many Ford jokes were the following:

What is a President Ford tongue twister? Answer: Hello.

Did you hear about the Jerry Ford doll? You wind it up and it lurches into something.

The only thing between [Vice President] Nelson Rockefeller and the presidency is a banana peel.

The Secret Service refused to let Ford throw out the first pitch for the baseball season because there was too much danger of his being beaned.[8]

Ford tried to show that he had a sense of humor about all the ridicule, and he worked the theme into some of his speeches. But the image was forever set of President Klutz, President Gaffe, and President Curly.

Ford's "ridicule problem" brought to mind other politicians who had been seriously disparaged in the national agenda of public controversy. In 1952, Richard Nixon was ridiculed for his slush fund of leftover campaign contributions when he was nominated for the vice-presidency on the Dwight Eisenhower, Republican ticket. This "Tricky Dick" reputation followed Nixon throughout his career and was reinforced by his operatives' break-in at Democratic National Committee headquarters in the Watergate Hotel. Republican Spiro T. Agnew was plucked out of national political obscurity by Richard Nixon in 1968 to become Nixon's running mate. In 1969, he became a national joke as covered by media and comedians.

Known only within his home state of Maryland as its governor, Agnew was chided for his lack of national name recognition by comedians and pack journalists. By 1970 there were Spiro Agnew T-shirts and Spiro Agnew Mickey Mouse–type watches. Stand-up comedians used Agnew's vice presidency as an example of how high a rambling buffoon could go in the United States.[9] News footage appeared with Agnew hitting his doubles partner in the back of the head in tennis, and video showed Agnew hitting poor golf shots. Agnew's verbal gaffes were reported and Agnew responded with an attack on the national news media for their unfair Vietnam War reporting and the trivializations of the Nixon administration's policies.

Although Ford was basically ridiculed for his physical clumsiness, and Nixon and Agnew were criticized on integrity grounds, the media and comedians changed directions in the late 1970s to ridicule President Jimmy Carter for his accent, his family, his policies, and his perceived lack of competence. Carter jokes focused on his political ineptness and his inability to lead the country in domestic and foreign affairs. Combined with negative press, this barrage of competency jokes from comedians made it difficult for Carter to command presidential respect.

During the 1980s, Ronald Reagan became a comedian's dream. Reagan's mistakes, gaffes, and policy foul-ups provided ammunition for the comedians. For some reason, the ridicule problem and the competency issue never hurt Reagan politically. His image as a strong leader was never really challenged by comedians and satirists in the court of public opinion. Reagan hired jokewriters himself and became like a stand-up comedian who was Master of Ceremonies for the 1980s.

He became the nation's top comedy activist as his carefully crafted one-liners dominated the sound-bite space on the national airwaves. Many suggested that he had the wit and humor of perhaps John F. Kennedy or Abraham

Lincoln, but these suggestions came mostly from Reagan "spin doctors."[10] Kennedy and Lincoln did not have to worry about cultivating one-liners for national ten-second sound bites to communicate to citizens on the national news. Moreover, Kennedy and Lincoln never hired joke-writers. A sampling of classic Reagan one-liners includes the following:

> I got an unsigned valentine, and I'm sure it was from Fritz Mondale. The heart on it was bleeding.

> Did you hear that the Communists now have a million-dollar lottery for their people? The winners get a dollar a year for a million years.

> [*Reagan was asked if he liked being president more than being a movie actor, he replied*] Yes, because here I get to write the script, too.

> [*To the doctors operating on him after the 1981 assassination attempt against his life*] I sure hope you're all Republicans.

> [*To Congress with respect to a possible veto of a bill*] Go ahead. Make my day.[11]

Much of the ridicule of the Reagan years came not so much from jokes about Reagan's manner, decision-making skills, age, or policies, but from Reagan's actual verbal gaffes during his presidency. Mark Green and Gail Mac-Coll published *There He Goes Again: Ronald Reagan's Reign of Error* in 1983 and started the phenomenon of the compilation of Reagan's unbelievable statements. Among Reagan's classic statements are the following:

> [*To aide Stuart Spencer in 1966*] Politics is just like show business. You have a hell of an opening, coast for a while, and then have a hell of a close.

> How can we abandon this country [*South Africa*] that has stood beside us in every war we've ever fought. (1981)

> There were two Vietnams, north and south. They had been separate nations for centuries. (1978)

> Approximately 80 percent of our air pollution stems from hydrocarbons released by vegetation, so let's not go overboard in setting and enforcing tough emission standards from man-made sources. (1980)[12]

Morton and Margaret Mintz continued compiling Reagan sayings and in 1986 they published *Quotations from President Ron*. Some of the major Reagan quotations from their book include the following:

> [*To Samuel Pierce, his only black cabinet member, 1986*] Hello, Mr. Mayor.

> [*On greeting boxer Sugar Ray Leonard and his wife at the White House in 1981*] We're proud to have Sugar Ray and Mrs. Ray here.

[*On laying a memorial wreath in Bitburg cemetery in 1985 to honor German soldiers and Nazi SS troopers*] They were victims, just as surely as the victims in the concentration camps.

[*When asked if he would visit the Vietnam War Memorial on Veteran's Day in 1982*] I can't tell until somebody tells me . . . I never know where I'm going.[13]

The Reagan years proved to be trend-setting as comedy writers recognized the politician's ability to write his own funny material by just quoting statements made by politicians. In 1989 writers Ken Brady and Jeremy Solomon published some of the collected gems of Reagan's successor in their *The Wit and Wisdom of George Bush*. The authors simply reported Bush's famous foot-in-mouth sayings to make a funny—and scary—comedy book. Among the best of George Bush's greatest gaffes are the following:

[*On touring the death camp at Auschwitz in 1987*] Boy, they were big on crematoriums weren't they?

[*On introducing his three half-Mexican grandchildren to the press on 1988 he called them*] The little brown ones over there.

[*Trying to invoke his famous "Thousand Points of Light" reference*] A thousand shining hill.

[*Describing his close relationship with Ronald Reagan in 1988*] For seven and a half years I have worked alongside him, and I am proud to be his partner. We have had triumphs, we have made mistakes, we have had sex . . . .

That's why I'll be a great conservative and environmental president. I plan to fish and hunt as much as I can.[14]

But no politician came up with better material than Bush's vice president, Dan Quayle. Comedians ridiculed Quayle to levels that surpassed the Ford and Agnew ridicule problems, but Quayle often provided the best material on himself. He said things such as the following:

[*Discussing the Holocaust with reporters in 1988*] The Holocaust was an obscene period in our nation's history. I mean this century's history. But we all lived in this century. I didn't live in this century.

Republicans understand the importance of the bondage between parent and child.[15]

Quayle was turned into a national joke mostly because of his incredible gaffes. There were Dan Quayle watches and T-shirts. A journal called the *Quayle Quarterly* popped up to chronicle Quayle's mistakes.

But the high priests of political comedy that can make or break a politician are the talk show hosts who do nightly current events monologues. These stand-up comedians with their nightly forum can engage in a comedic feeding frenzy and destroy a politician with the accumulative weight of their pointed jokes. Senator Gary Hart dropped out of the running of the 1988 presidential election sweepstakes although he was the front-runner in 1987 not so much because of his alleged extramarital affair with Donna Rice, but because he had become a national joke.

At every copying machine in the United States and during every coffee break, people all across the country would regale fellow employees with the latest Gary Hart jokes:

What was Hart's favorite dessert? Rice pudding.

I guess Hart took this acting Kennedyesque a little too far.

At least Hart is not like all the other politicians, he didn't screw the country, yet.

In 1984 the media made a big deal out of the fact that Gary Hart had changed his name from his birthname of Hartpence to Hart when he went to college. Well, in 1987, I guess the media was correct after all. If Hart hadn't dropped his "pence," he still might have had a chance to be president.

When Johnny Carson retired from *The Tonight Show* in 1992 after doing thirty years of monologues, he left behind the standard for talk show hosts to follow in their nightly topical humor.[16] Carson had scored national points with some anti–Vietnam War humor in the early 1970s, some brilliant Nixon–Watergate jokes, Ford and Carter jokes, Reagan impressions, blistering Iran-Contra humor, Hart jokes, and Bush and Quayle comments.

Jay Leno became Carson's replacement in 1992 and his monologues were even more political than Carson's. Arsenio Hall provided hip humor about the political system during his opening set. David Letterman and his staff of writers plastered politicians in the 1980s and 1990s on *Late Night with David Letterman* and Dennis Miller provided political comedy on his talk show for the thinking man and woman. Kevin Nealon read his political humor on the *Saturday Night Live* newscasts, which often set the tone for political humor in the early 1990s. A sampling of some of their better material might include the following:

[*Jay Leno on Bill Clinton's war record*] People said Clinton . . . was afraid to go to war . . . That's unfair. He stood a much greater chance of getting shot here at home by a jealous husband.

[*Dennis Miller on Clinton*] I think it's ironic that Vietnam was the only time this guy didn't see any action.

[*Kevin Nealon on Clinton*] On a scale of 1–10, Gennifer Flowers gave presidential hopeful Bill Clinton a nine as a lover. She said it would have been a ten, except he had no health care plan.

[Johnny Carson on Gennifer Flowers' rating Clinton a nine] The Japanese prime minister said if Clinton had a stronger work ethic, he'd have been a ten.[17]

The 2000 election was a gold mine for political humorists due to the obvious possibilities of the two presidential candidates. *Saturday Night Live* lampooned George W. Bush for mangling words and not being very bright, while Al Gore was caricatured as stiff and programmed. One satire of their televised debates pictured Will Ferrell playing an overwhelmed Bush whispering, "I pass," in response to a question he didn't understand.

Darrell Hammond meanwhile portrayed a completely humorless Gore who shoehorns the word *lockbox* into every answer (in honor of his pledge to safeguard the sanctity of the Social Security surplus). Sighing deeply before every answer, similar to the way the candidate had done during the first presidential debate, Hammond showed a Gore who was devoid of humanity and utterly incapable of any serious emotion.

Demonstrating that each candidate understood the virtue of self-parody, Bush made a cameo appearance in which he announced he was "ambilavent" about being on the episode due to its "offensible" material. Not wanting to be outdone, Gore announced, "I was one of the very first to be offended by material on *Saturday Night Live*." Appearing on ABC's *Nightline* and referring to his sighing during the debates, Gore joked, "I've put all my sighs in a lockbox."[18]

Following Bush's victory in the Electoral College after a disputed ballot count in Florida, late night comedians continued their onslaught on the Texas governor. Comics averaged forty jokes per night about "electoral dysfunction." Nearly half of the jokes were told at the expense of Florida residents for their inability to punch holes properly in the ballot. Bush and Gore, respectively, were the objects of the remainder of the humorous comments. Jay Leno, for example, joked in regard to the Sunshine State that, "I haven't seen people in Florida this mad since Metamucil switched to a childproof cap."[19]

There even was a book titled *George W. Bushisms: The Accidental Wit and Wisdom of Our 43rd President* that examined the president's tendency to fracture language and convey thoughts different from what he intended.[20] The volume printed the following gems from George W. Bush:

It's clearly a budget. It's got a lot of numbers in it. (p. 37)

One of the common denominators I have found is that expectations rise above that which is expected. (p. 68)

If you're sick and tired of the politics of cynicism and polls and principles, come and join this campaign. (p. 14)

I do know I'm ready for the job. And if not, that's just the way it goes. (p. 14)

They misunderestimated me. (p. 22)

I think if you know what you believe, it makes it a lot easier to answer questions. I can't answer your question. (p. 26).

One joke that circulated through e-mail made fun of Bush's reputation for not being very smart. The commentary went as follows:

Einstein dies and goes to Heaven. At the Pearly Gates, Saint Peter tells him, "You look like Einstein, but you have NO idea the lengths that some people will go to in order to sneak into Heaven. Can you prove who you really are?" Einstein ponders for a few seconds and asks, "Could I have a blackboard and some chalk?" Saint Peter snaps his fingers and a blackboard and chalk instantly appear. Einstein proceeds to fill the board with arcane mathematical equations. Saint Peter is suitably impressed. "You really ARE Einstein!" he says. "Welcome to Heaven!" The next to arrive is Picasso. Once again, Saint Peter asks for credentials. Picasso asks, "Mind if I use that blackboard and chalk?" Saint Peter says, "Go ahead." Picasso erases Einstein's equations and sketches a truly stunning mural with just a few strokes of chalk. Saint Peter claps. "Surely you are the great artist you claim to be!" he says. "Come on in!" Then Saint Peter looks up and sees George W. Bush. Saint Peter scratches his head and says, "Einstein and Picasso both managed to prove their identity. How can you prove yours?" George W. looks bewildered and says, "Who are Einstein and Picasso?" Saint Peter sighs and says, "Come on in, George."

A few months into his presidency, President Bush responded by making fun of himself at the Washington Gridiron Club. "Those stories about my intellectual capacity do get under my skin. You know for a while I even thought my staff believed it," he said. "There on my schedule first thing every morning it said, 'Intelligence briefing.'"[21] Later, at a White House event honoring baseball legends such as Yogi Berra, Bush announced, "Yogi's been an inspiration to me—not only because of his baseball skills, but of course for the enduring mark he left on the English language. Some of the press corps even think he might be my speechwriter."[22]

In her successful bid for the U.S. Senate, Hillary Clinton became the object of sexist jokes. Given the range of emotions stirred by a strong woman seeking to make history by being the only first lady to win an election in her own right, it is little surprise that her candidacy generated caustic humor. One biting commentary, for example, called the "Hillary Chicken Dinner" ridiculed her personal appearance in an extremely tasteless manner. At the price of $4.95, the dinner was advertised as consisting of "two small breasts, two left wings, and two large thighs."[23]

Through these jokes, satires, and monologues, it became apparent that not only have stand-up comedians become political activists via the impact of their political jokes, but also they help shape the manner in which prominent politicians are seen. A number of presidents from Ford and Reagan to Clinton and George W. Bush saw negative public profiles of themselves built in substantial part through the jokes told at their expense. The images created through these comedy routines affected the rise and fall of their political fortunes.

One comedian, Pat Paulsen, even became a perennial self-proclaimed candidate for president. Paulsen made fun of politicians in his routines and then outlined in comedic fashion what he would do as president of the United States. For example, he noted that "attending the Gerald R. Ford Symposium on 'Humor and the Presidency,' is sort of like attending the Ayatollah Khomeini Symposium on the sexual revolution."[24]

This interplay between comedians and the political system keeps citizens entertained while watching American politics. It is a way to boost public interest in a subject about which many Americans are not deeply absorbed. The idea is that politics doesn't hurt as much if you are laughing at public officials.

Unfortunately, in celebrity politics humor is used too often to trivialize important national issues and politicians. Rather than using humor to engage the public in serious substantive issues, humor deflects from substance and draws our attention to personal or trivial aspects of the political process. When voters form impressions based on comedian monologues, it risks debasing the civic discourse. In these ways, then, humor has political consequences that can affect campaigns and governing.

NOTES

1. Bruce Granger, *Political Satire in the American Revolution, 1763–1783* (Ithaca, NY: Cornell University Press, 1960), p. 1.
2. Darrell M. West, *The Rise and Fall of the Media Establishment* (Boston: Bedford/St. Martin's Press, 2001).
3. Quoted in John Bartlett, *Familiar Quotations*, 10th ed. (Boston: Little, Brown, 1919). Reported in on-line version at www.bartleby.com under *Mark Twain*.
4. Will Rogers, "A Politician Is Not as Narrow-Minded as He Forces Himself to Be," *New York Herald*, 26 August 1876. Quoted on Web site, www.twainquotes.com.
5. Ralph J. Gleason, "Lenny Bruce at the Turning Point," *Rolling Stone*, 26 October 1972, pp. 32–33.
6. Jim Rutenberg, "Impersonator in Chief Is No Bush Supporter," *Providence Journal*, 3 February 2001, p. D-1.
7. "The Ridicule Problem," *Time*, 5 January 1976, p. 33.
8. "The Ridicule Problem," *Time*, 5 January 1976, p. 33.
9. Henry Beck, "Spiro Agnew: The Fool." Paper presented at the Annual Meeting of the American Political Science Association, Washington, D.C., September 3, 1977.
10. See Bill Adler, ed., *The Kennedy Wit* (New York: Citadel Press, 1964) and Max Stein, ed., *Abe Lincoln's Jokes* (Chicago: Stein Publishers, 1943).
11. See William Troxler, *Along Wit's Trail: The Humor and Wisdom of Ronald Reagan* (New York: Holt, Rinehart and Winston, 1983), pp. 24–36, and see Mark Knoller, "Reagan Keeps Everyone Laughing," *Bridgeport Post*, 24 August 1986, p. B-9.
12. Mark Green and Gail MacColl, *There He Goes Again: Ronald Reagan's Reign of Error* (New York: Pantheon, 1983), pp. 8, 24, 32, and 99.
13. Morton Mintz and Margaret Mintz, *Quotations from President Ron* (London: Futura Publications, 1986), pp. 8, 9, 35, and 55.

14. Ken Brady and Jeremy Solomon, *The Wit and Wisdom of George Bush* (New York: St. Martin's Press, 1989), pp. 19, 22, 25, 27, 80, and 81.
15. *Quayle Quarterly* (winter 1990).
16. Frank Rich, "So Long to Johnny, America's Sandman," *New York Times*, 10 May 1992, Arts and Leisure section 2, pp. 1, 26.
17. *USA Today*, "In Quotes," 14 February 1992, p. 7-A.
18. Caryn James, "Where Politics and Comedy Intermingle, the Punch Lines Can Draw Blood," *New York Times*, 4 November 2000, p. A-21.
19. Information from Center for Media and Public Affairs Web site at www.cmpa.com.
20. Jacob Weisberg, ed., *George W. Bushisms: The Accidental Wit and Wisdom of Our 43rd President* (New York: Fireside, 2001).
21. Ron Fournier, "Bush's Speech Steals the Show," *Providence Journal*, 26 March 2001, p. A-2.
22. *Providence Journal*, "Domestic Policy: T-Ball for All at White House," 1 April 2001, p. A-9.
23. *New York Daily News*, "The Buzz," 29 August 2000, p. 4.
24. Andrew Malcolm, "At 2-Day Symposium, It's Hail to Chiefs for Pratfalls and Belly Laughs," *New York Times*, 19 September 1986, p. 11 and Elizabeth Kastor, "To Wit, Ford & the Funnymen," *Washington Post*, 19 September 1986, p. D-1.

PUBLIC EVALUATIONS
OF THE CELEBRITY REGIME

In many respects, the American public is quite supportive of a regime based on celebrity politics. Tabloid newspapers have a large circulation. For example, the *National Enquirer* sells around 2.3 million copies every week and the *Star* has a circulation of 1.7 million. Television shows devoted to gossip about the famous do well. An average of 3.5 million watch the syndicated television show *Inside Edition* each day and the E entertainment network attracts several million viewers to its various shows about Hollywood and celebrity profiles.[1]

National surveys document that around 10 percent of Americans get information about national politics from late-night entertainment shows such as the *Tonight Show* starring Jay Leno and *Late Night with David Letterman*. For those under the age of thirty years old, this figure rises to nearly half. As the network news has emphasized entertainment features and lifestyle stories at the expense of hard news, more and more Americans have turned to entertainment shows for political commentary.[2]

Popular culture competes successfully with politics in the lives of many Americans. For example, after Clinton's affair with Monica Lewinsky hit the airwaves, polls revealed that as many parents that year reported they were discussing with their kids the competitive home run derby between baseball stars Sammy Sosa and Mark McGwire as the Lewinsky affair.[3] It was a sign of how much public interest there is in high-profile athletes compared to issues associated with the country's civic life.

New "reality-based" television shows such as *Survivor, Temptation Island, Who Wants To Be a Millionaire?* and *Who Wants to Marry a Multi-Millionaire?* have become wildly popular with viewers. The final episode of the first season of *Survivor* earned ratings that were second only to the Super Bowl.

Proving that this was no fluke, opening shows in the second season of *Survivor*, set in the Australian outback, attracted nearly 30 million watchers. This series was especially popular among young viewers under the age of thirty-five, a demographic group that traditionally did not watch the major networks in large numbers.[4]

The popularity of this genre led pollsters to ask a national sample what they would be willing to allow a reality-based television show to film them doing. The most popular results were 31 percent for being in their pajamas, 29 percent for kissing, 26 percent for crying, 25 percent having an argument with someone, 16 percent being drunk, 10 percent eating a rat or an insect, 8 percent being naked, and 5 percent having sex.[5]

It is possible that the intimacy of reality-based programs have inured viewers to invasions of privacy and conditioned them to accept the instant celebrity of ordinary people, such as Richard Hatch of *Survivor* fame.

Celebrities, musicians, sports figures, and movie stars are among the most recognized people in America. Personalities such as Madonna, Kathie Lee, Roseanne, Prince, and Cher are so famous that they are known by their first names only. Other prominent figures have become mass merchandising conglomerates, complete with fan clubs, newsletters, best-selling books, and a wide array of consumer products from T-shirts and blue jeans to sports clothes. Rush Limbaugh sells ties, newsletters, and books to his adoring public who have taken on the name "ditto heads" in honor of their tendency to reiterate his viewpoints.[6] Kathie Lee Gifford markets her own line of clothing. Tim Allen once had the best-selling book, and the most popular movie and television show at the same time, a feat that is unrivaled in modern times.[7]

The rise of the Internet has provided new opportunities for the glorification of celebrities. On-line fan clubs have proliferated as have chat rooms devoted to particular celebrities. One now can find virtual communities that share information about leading figures or trade gossip about popular television shows. Regardless of whether one's interests lie in music, sports, politics, television, or movies, there is a Web site that will put you in touch with like-minded souls interested in sharing your obsession.

For example, on yahoo.com, there are on-line clubs devoted to soap opera queen Susan Lucci, rock star Rod Stewart, actress Bette Midler, basketball star Karl Malone, and many other celebrities from the worlds of music, acting, and sports. Surfers can sign up as "official members" of the fan club and endlessly swap information about their favorite celebrity.[8] Sometimes this obsession with celebrity is taken to the extreme of stalking famous people.

National surveys avidly track public rankings of top movie stars. In 2000, for example, a Harris Poll showed the country's most favorite stars were Harrison Ford, John Wayne, Mel Gibson, Julia Roberts, and Clint Eastwood. A similar rating of top television personalities revealed fan favorites to be Oprah Winfrey, Regis Philbin, Drew Carey, Jerry Seinfeld, and Kelsey Grammer.[9] Such rankings generate intense disputes among fans when particular celebrities do less well than their supporters believe is warranted.

The stars of sports, business, and entertainment achieve a level of prominence that rivals that of major American politicians. For example, of the top individuals who in 2000 could be correctly identified by their countrymen with particular jobs, the top two (Al Gore and George W. Bush) were presidential candidates who were spending millions to build name identification, but the next most recognizable people were Regis Philbin (the host of the ABC show *Who Wants to Be a Millionaire?*), golfer Tiger Woods, Microsoft Chairman Bill Gates, and NBC *Tonight* show host Jay Leno.[10]

In addition to their high name identification, celebrities dominate lists of personalities young people most would like to encounter. A national survey recently asked teenagers which type of person they most would like to meet. Fitting an era that idolizes entertainment and sports celebrities, this study found that the largest percentage of young people named musicians, while the next most popular individuals were athletes and actors, respectively.[11] Politicians ranked well down the list of preferred introductions.

Befitting their fall from grace, conventional politicians rank down with used car salespeople in public trustworthiness and respect. Lists of professions in which the public has a great deal of confidence find clergy, teachers, and doctors at the top of the list, while politicians, salespeople, and realtors clustered at the bottom.[12] The old days when public officials were heroes and respected figures has ended. In its place is an era of widespread cynicism and mistrust on the part of the general public.

Even though Americans tend not to trust politicians, they have greater respect for and confidence in celebrities who enter the world of politics, especially legacies and famed nonpoliticos. These individuals have a fame that transcends public service and a reputation for honesty and personal integrity. This allows them to succeed politically in ways that are unavailable to more conventional kinds of politicos.[13]

In the electoral realm, for example, citizens have a well-documented tendency to vote for celebrity politicians. First Lady Hillary Clinton was elected to the U.S. Senate from New York without any previous personal service in elective office. Former pro-wrestler Jesse Ventura shocked the experts by winning the Minnesota governor's office (and then he wrote a best-selling book).[14] A variety of sports stars have become successful public officials in the House and Senate.

As demonstrated previously, these celebrities are adept at dealing with the media and are adroit fund-raisers. Ted Kennedy's son, Congressman Patrick Kennedy of Rhode Island, has been among the most popular officeholders within that state and a successful fund-raiser to boot. During the 2000 elections, Patrick Kennedy's last name helped him raise $97 million for the Democratic Congressional Campaign Committee in an unsuccessful effort to win the House back for Democrats.[15]

Based on these and other examples discussed in this research, it is clear that the cult of personality is alive and well throughout our society, culture, and political system.[16] Prominent individuals occupy a special niche in public life and as the line between Hollywood and Washington has blurred, they have managed to enter the political process in large numbers and do surprisingly well. Indeed, in many respects, the trends toward media domination of politics, the rise of expensive campaigns, and the need for leaders who are trusted has facilitated the entry of the rich and famous into national life.

Yet despite our celebrity-crazed culture, there are warning signs on the horizon of a backlash against celebrity politics, and the media, scandal, and big money associated with it. Americans are tired of scandal politics geared to celebrity gossip and investigations into personal background. The aftermath of GOP investigations into the private life of President Bill Clinton produced bitterness and anger toward Republicans.[17] Bucking the traditional tendency of the party controlling the presidency to lose seats in midterm elections, Democrats actually gained House seats in 1998. When he left office, Clinton had a historically high job approval rating (at least until he pardoned several controversial individuals).

Citizens increasingly have become upset with how mass media cover the news in a scandal-riddled era. At the time of the Senate impeachment trial of President Clinton, only 35 percent of Americans said they thought reporters had done a good job covering the trial.[18] A 1998 national survey revealed that 55 percent believed media coverage of the Lewinsky scandal in general had been only fair or poor, while 42 percent felt it had been good.[19]

In these episodes as well as in coverage of politics more generally, viewers think that the press goes overboard on prominent news events and produces reporting that is inaccurate. News organizations used to be trusted far more than they are today in delivering information to the general public. In 1985, for example, 55 percent of people across the country felt news organizations generally got the facts correct in stories. A decade later, public confidence had dropped considerably. Fifty-six percent of Americans believed news stories often were inaccurate.[20] This is a dangerous sign that the public is losing confidence in the press as an institution.

In the contemporary period, citizen dissatisfaction with common investigative reporting is high. When asked about various news techniques, 52 percent said they approved of using stories with unnamed sources, 42 percent supported relying on hidden cameras and microphones, 31 percent favored journalists not identifying themselves as reporters, and 29 percent favored paying informers for news information.[21]

These results are revealing because they are the very techniques that have become common in a media obsessed with political scandal and tabloid coverage of personal background. Reliance on anonymous sources has risen dramatically, even among the mainstream press outlets that used to abhor relying on unnamed sources. As the line between news and entertainment breaks down, it becomes harder for readers and viewers to distinguish fact from fiction in news reporting and to respect the new norms that govern press behavior in terms of information gathering.

The public, furthermore, has expressed revulsion against so-called Hollywood values that glorify sex and violence in movies, videos, music, and television. Rather than accepting the idea that the entertainment industry should be allowed to produce whatever the market is willing to support, large numbers of Americans support the view that popular culture is going downhill and that something should be done about it. For example, 66 percent of Americans believe that society's standards for acceptable and unacceptable behavior have become lower in recent years. The same national survey found that 60 percent think it is more important to promote greater respect for traditional values than to encourage greater tolerance of people with different lifestyles and backgrounds.[22]

Taking off on then Vice President Dan Quayle's attacks on the Hollywood cultural elite, many people have discussed the need for higher moral standards and more civil discourse in American society. Writers such as William Bennett have decried the prevalence of sex and violence in our culture and the necessity of cultural leaders to take greater social responsibility for what they produce.[23] A country cannot maintain greatness, according to these proponents, unless it retains its moral center.

Public opinion polls demonstrate that many Americans worry about the current content of popular culture. Overall, 62 percent of Americans find negative racial stereotypes in movies as very offensive, 54 percent object to graphic violence, and 38 percent believe that nudity in movies is very offensive. These numbers are in keeping with the growing view that something fundamental is wrong with a society that shows violence without consequences during prime-time entertainment shows on television.

However, reflecting the diversity of the United States, there is a gender and age gap in some of these attitudes. Women are more likely than men to object to graphic violence, profanity, and gender stereotypes. Young people are less likely than older Americans to complain about movies and television shows containing nudity and sexual content.[24]

Perhaps no episode illustrated the backlash against tabloidization and celebrity politics better than the death of Princess Diana in a Paris car accident. As a sign of how people feel personally touched by prominent personalities, more than half of the British and a quarter of Americans (27 percent) said they felt as upset about her death as they would if someone they knew had died. Sixty-three percent of American women and 38 percent of American men indicated they were "fans" of Princess Diana.[25] These were remarkably high levels of support for a member of the British royalty from a country that rejected that form of government.

The role that tabloid journalists played in hounding the Princess throughout her adult life and the practice of hiring cars that would follow

Diana's vehicle at high rates of speed led large numbers of citizens to blame the tabloids for her fatal car accident. Would she have died, critics asked, if photographers and tabloid reporters had not constantly followed her around? Such hounding represents the down-side of a celebrity culture that craves every last detail about the private lives of the rich and famous. Many wondered if the tabloid press indeed bore some responsibility for the car accident that killed Princess Diana.[26]

In order to find out how people felt about this, polls in the United States and Great Britain asked a national sample of respondents in each country whether they felt the tabloids bore some responsibility for her death. The results were stunning. Sixty percent of Americans felt the tabloids were very or extremely responsible for the accident that killed her, while in Great Britain, 64 percent felt that way.[27] The numbers represented clear evidence that a tabloid backlash was emerging in both nations.

Based on these impressions of the circumstances surrounding her death, large numbers of citizens in both countries concluded that it was time to take dramatic action to protect celebrities. For example, 80 percent of respondents in the United States and Great Britain concluded that it was more important to protect the privacy of celebrities than for the public to have a right to know about the personal lives of famous individuals. In other words, the tabloid media clearly had gone too far in the eyes of the general public, and it was time to impose some restrictions on the ability of reporters to hound famous people.

In addition, a majority believed that celebrities deserved special protection from paparazzi photographers who pursued them in search of candid celebrity photos. Rather than being fair game for whomever wanted to track them down, prominent politicians and entertainers had some rights, too, from overly intrusive members of the press corps.

To show that such views were not mere rhetoric on the part of the general public, many Americans indicated they would support a press boycott unless changes were made. When asked about the manner in which celebrities were covered, 45 percent of Americans said they would support boycotts of tabloid press outlets in order to bring about changes in how the media dealt with celebrity figures.[28] This added teeth to the views expressed earlier in national public opinion surveys.

A similar reaction developed in 1999 following the death of John Kennedy, Jr., in a tragic plane crash. As investigators searched for the downed plane, a riveted nation watched television for hours at a time. Commentators analyzed the impact of the Kennedys on American public life and the 24-hour news organizations devoted several days to the search, recovery, and memorial for the young Kennedy.[29]

After Kennedy's plane was found at the bottom of the ocean, polls found that 19 percent of Americans indicated they were as upset as if a member of their own family had died and another 74 percent said they felt sad about the event. Women were more likely than men to react negatively to Kennedy's death. The same was true for senior citizens of both sexes.[30]

Media reporting about the private lives of prominent families such as the Kennedys is so pervasive that people consider the family people they actually know and care about. Just as marriages and political successes are celebrated, so, too, are deaths and tragedies mourned. It is a vivid demonstration of how celebrity status pervades America's conceptions about itself and people's views about their own societal attachments.[31]

Such incidents—the death of Princess Diana and the plane crash of John Kennedy, Jr.—demonstrate both the considerable public interest that remains in prominent personalities, and the concerns citizens feel about media coverage of celebrities. In response to a national poll, 81 percent of Americans said they followed the story about Kennedy's tragic plane crash either very or somewhat closely. This figure was among the highest of any news story that had taken place over the past decade, putting it on par with the death of Princess Diana and the start of the Gulf War in the Middle East.[32]

However, more than half (58 percent) of those surveyed indicated that they thought the amount of media coverage devoted to the Kennedy plane crash was excessive, compared to 49 percent who felt that way about coverage of the death of Princess Diana.[33] At the same time that the public consumes the celebrity regime in large numbers, it is ambivalent about what this means for the celebrities themselves and the consequences for our culture and society.

Even before Senator John McCain appeared on the presidential election scene to make a big issue of campaign finance reform, a variety of national opinion surveys demonstrated that large numbers of Americans see money as having gained excessive influence in American politics. The fear is that secret money from large contributors is corrupting our polity and allowing small groups of well-connected donors to gain disproportionate influence.[34]

Given these concerns, it is not surprising that 64 percent of Americans believe federal campaign finance laws should be completely overhauled or changed in major ways. Only 8 percent believe the current system is "fine as is." Seventy-two percent report that they favor new laws limiting the amount of large "soft money" gifts that can be contributed legally to national political parties.[35]

It has been a common tenet of American politics to fear the corrupting power of big money in American politics. At the turn of the twentieth century, muckrakers bemoaned the bribery and extortion that was common on the local, state, and national scene. Numerous press stories exposed wrongdoing in high places and the crucial role that secret money played in distorting representational linkages in American politics.

The same fears are present today. Growing loopholes in campaign finance laws have allowed large amounts of secret money to reenter our political system. Large organizations from a variety of political persuasions—business, union, and social issue—contest both elections and policymaking, and use money to advance narrow interests.[36]

Since celebrities are an important vehicle for the solicitation of political money, they bear some responsibility for the discontent surrounding the entire money-in-politics controversy. It is not possible to address public concerns in this area without dealing with issue advocacy supported by Hollywood figures (such as Jane Fonda's $12 million contribution to abortion rights organizations) or soft money contributions provided by entertainment interests from Dreamworks to Rupert Murdoch's various organizations.[37]

Another recent event that revealed fissures in the system of celebrity politics that has emerged in the United States concerns the controversies over former President Clinton's pardons at the end of his term. In what many viewed as the ultimate combination of celebrityhood, campaign fund-raising, and political actions, Clinton pardoned fugitive financier Marc Rich after his former wife, songwriter Denise Rich, gave hundreds of thousands of dollars in contributions to the Democratic national party and the Clinton library.[38]

The effort to achieve this pardon was organized with the precision of a military operation. In the closing days of his administration, Denise Rich wrote a letter to Clinton asking for the pardon, called the president, and spoke with him about it at a White House party. One observer at this social occasion claimed that Rich talked to Clinton only "after wrestling him away from Barbra Streissand," who also was in attendance at this party. In conjunction with one of Clinton's top fund-raisers, Beth Dozoretz, a close friend of Denise Rich's, the White House was bombarded with calls and e-mails supporting Rich's pardon. One communication noted that most of Clinton's lawyers and people in the Justice Department were opposed to the pardon, and that somehow Clinton hoped to find a way around this opposition.[39]

After Marc Rich hired former Clinton counsel Jack Quinn, a string of religious, political, and cultural contacts were used to urge Clinton to pardon Rich. Individuals such as Israeli prime minister Ehud Barak, Elie Wiesel, and Shimon Peres wrote letters on behalf of Rich noting that the man had given millions of dollars in charitable contributions to needy organizations in Israel and elsewhere. In the waning days of his administration, Clinton pardoned Rich and unleashed a national furor over the action. The pardon led to weeks of unfavorable news coverage for the former president and an extensive investigation by the House and Senate.

It was not the only pardon that shed light on the close connection between money, fame, and political decision making. Close Clinton friend Harry Thomason, the Hollywood producer of the television show *Designing Women*, contacted Clinton seeking pardons for James Manning and Robert Fain. Thomason, who produced a video about Clinton for the 1992 presidential campaign, called Clinton about the pardons and directed friends of the individuals seeking the actions to contact former Clinton aide Harold Ickes. According to one lawyer, Thomason "was prepared to put his name and reputation on the line in support of these two individuals." Given Thomason's close personal friendship with Clinton, this individual said, "That's an important endorsement of the two of them."[40] Shortly thereafter, both men received presidential pardons.

Six months earlier, Hollywood and Washington had intersected at another point during the Clinton White House. According to one news story, Thomason had a million-dollar dispute with the CBS television network over past series proposal deals that had not panned out. CBS owed Thomason around $3 million but had not paid the bill. Leslie Moonves, CBS television president, said that before Clinton left office, he received a call from the chief executive asking Moonves to "be nice" to Thomason and noting that Thomason was "our friend." Although Moonves denied that the call had influenced his decision, CBS did pay Thomason the money owed after its president received the Clinton phone call.[41]

To summarize, the public is ambivalent about the close intertwining of celebrityhood, money, media, and politics that have emerged in the United States. On the one hand, people read and watch tabloid news shows in large numbers and pay close attention to personal information about the rich and famous. They glorify celebrities and want to know every last detail about them. Fan clubs are popular and on-line chat rooms are crowded with gossip about these high-profile individuals.

However, on the other hand, there is growing public concern about the tabloidization of the American media and the culture of celebrityhood that pervades our society. Many people worry that our country has gone overboard on celebrities, that we routinely invade their privacy, and that we sometimes even endanger their lives. Far from embracing this celebrity regime, a variety of polls and other indicators demonstrate that there is a backlash against it. Celebrities deserve some privacy, and the media coverage and tabloidization associated with them is considered quite problematic by the American public.

There is also growing concern about the dominant role of big money in American politics. The increased interest in campaign finance reform reflects the fear of many Americans that rich celebrities and others with private agendas have undue influence over elected officials. This perception contributes to public distrust of politicians and of the political system. Until we address this issue, it will be difficult to resolve some of the major dilemmas of our current political situation.

NOTES

1. *Ulrich's International Periodicals Directory* (New York: Bowker, 2000).
2. Paul Brownfield, "Iowa, New Hampshire . . . 'Tonight Show'?" *Los Angeles Times,* 11 February 2000 and Don Aucoin, "McCain and Bush Take to the Late Night Airwaves," *Boston Globe,* 1 March 2000, p. F-1.

3. Pew Research Center for the People & the Press, "White House Scandal Has Families Talking," press release, September 1998, p. 2.
4. Bill Carter, "Successes of Reality TV Put Networks in 'Survivor' Mode," *New York Times*, 3 February 2001, p. A-1.
5. CNN/Time Poll conducted June 14–15, 2000. Reported at www.pollingreport.com.
6. Rush Limbaugh, *The Way Things Ought To Be* (New York: Pocket Books, 1992).
7. Tim Allen, *Don't Stand Too Close to a Naked Man* (New York: Hyperion, 1994).
8. These fan clubs can be found at www.yahoo.com, under *Entertainment and Clubs*.
9. Harris Poll conducted October 19–26, 2000. Reported at www.pollingreport.com.
10. Gallup Poll conducted January 25–26, 2000. Reported at www.gallup.com.
11. *Business Week*, "Inventors Are, Like, Yucky and Stuff," 5 February 2001, p. 69.
12. Seymour Martin Lipset and William Schneider, *The Confidence Gap*, rev. ed. (Baltimore: Johns Hopkins University Press, 1987).
13. David Canon, *Actors, Athletes, and Astronauts* (Chicago: University of Chicago Press, 1990).
14. Jesse Ventura, *I Ain't Got Time to Bleed: Reworking the Body Politic from the Bottom Up* (New York: Villard, 1999).
15. Darrell M. West, *Patrick Kennedy: The Rise to Power* (Englewood Cliffs, NJ: Prentice Hall, 2000).
16. David Marshall, *Celebrity and Power: Fame in Contemporary Culture* (Minneapolis: University of Minnesota Press, 1997) and Ronald Brownstein, *The Power and the Glitter: The Hollywood–Washington Connection* (New York: Pantheon Books, 1990).
17. Howard Kurtz, *Spin Cycle* (New York: Free Press, 1998).
18. Pew Research Center for the People & the Press, "Senate Trial: Little Viewership, Little Impact," press release, January 18, 1999, p. 1
19. Pew Research Center for the People & the Press, "Democratic Congressional Changes Helped by Clinton Ratings," press release, April 3, 1998, p. 5.
20. Pew Research Center for the People & the Press, "Fewer Favor Media Scrutiny of Political Leaders," press release, March 21, 1997, p. 1.
21. Darrell M. West, *The Rise and Fall of the Media Establishment* (Boston: Bedford/St. Martin's Press, 2001), p. 105.
22. NBC News/*Wall Street Journal* Poll conducted June 16–19, 1999. Reported at www.pollingreport.com.
23. William Bennett, *The Book of Virtues: A Treasury of Great Moral Stories* (New York: Simon & Schuster, 1993).
24. Gallup Poll conducted July 16–18, 1999. Reported at www.gallup.com.
25. Gallup Poll conducted September 4, 1997 in both countries. Reported at www.gallup.com.
26. Christopher Anderson, *The Day Diana Died* (New York: William Morrow, 1998).
27. Gallup Poll conducted September 4, 1997 in both countries. Reported at www.gallup.com.
28. Gallup Poll conducted September 4, 1997 in both countries. Reported at www.gallup.com.
29. Christopher Anderson, *The Day John Died* (New York: William Morrow, 2000).
30. Gallup Poll conducted July 22–25, 1999. Reported at www.gallup.com.
31. Doris Kearns Goodwin, *The Fitzgeralds and the Kennedys* (New York: Simon & Schuster, 1987).
32. Gallup Poll conducted July 22–25, 1999. Reported at www.gallup.com.

33. Gallup Poll conducted July 22–25, 1999. Reported at www.gallup.com.

34. Darrell M. West, *Checkbook Democracy: How Money Corrupts Our Political System* (Boston: Northeastern University Press, 2000).

35. Gallup Poll conducted October 8–10, 1999. Reported at www.gallup.com.

36. Darrell M. West, *Checkbook Democracy: How Money Corrupts Our Political System* (Boston: Northeastern University Press, 2000).

37. Campaign finance reports can be found at the Center for Responsive Politics Web site at www.opensecrets.org.

38. Michiko Kakutan, "With the Guy Next Door in the Oval Office, the Presidency Shrinks Further," *New York Times*, 19 January 2001, p. A-17.

39. Alison Cowan, "Documents Show a Complex Campaign to Win a Pardon," *New York Times*, 10 February 2001, p. A-9.

40. David Johnston, "Hollywood Friend Had Clinton's Ear for Two Late Pardons," *New York Times*, 24 February 2001, p. A-8.

41. Bill Carter, "CBS TV Chief Says Clinton Did Not Influence a Deal," *New York Times*, 28 February 2001, p. A-17.

Heroes, Fools, and Villains in Celebrity Politics

America's celebrity politics makes for an entertaining show. We have political newsworthies whose lives are covered as if they were entertainers. There are famed nonpoliticos who raise money, endorse politicians, and sometimes even run for office themselves. Legacies who once might have been treated as intellectually deficient are treated as oracles for society. Event celebrities now help set the national agenda as to what is important politically to discuss. In other words, we see the full gambit of celebrities who serve as heroes, fools, and villains in American society.[1]

At one level, this celebrity regime can be beneficial to our political system. At least in the abstract, it offers the potential to reinvigorate American politics by introducing new blood and new ideas. Unlike conventional politicians, celebrities do not have to serve lengthy apprenticeships before they can run for major offices. They typically are less beholden to vested political interests because of their own wealth or ability to raise money from friends and family members. In a political world where entangling alliances are the rule, these kinds of individuals are as close to autonomous free agents as one can find in the American political process.

This freedom allows them to challenge the conventional wisdom, adopt unpopular stances, and expand the range of ideas that are represented in our national dialogue. It is no accident that Senator John McCain took the unconventional course of challenging his party's stance on campaign finance and tobacco regulation. As a former prisoner of war with a compelling personal story, he had greater autonomy to transcend party lines than often is the case.

The same pattern is true with the Kennedys. Other politicians have been ridiculed as hopeless liberals for taking positions designed to help the poor and downtrodden. Michael Dukakis was lambasted by George Herbert Walker Bush for political views that were left of center. However, because the Kennedy celebrityhood makes it possible for Senator Edward Kennedy to forge personal alliances with key Republicans such as Orrin Hatch and John McCain, Kennedy has thrived in the Senate despite the country's drift to the right.[2]

Event celebrities, legacies, and famed nonpoliticos are among the most trusted public figures in the country. They are not seen in the mistrusting way that most politicians are viewed by the public. Rather than having spent a lifetime cutting deals with other politicians, they have leapfrogged the political crowd and in the process carved out considerable flexibility for themselves in terms of their personal images.

Seen in this light, celebrities offer a means to reinvigorate a political process that often stagnates, is unable to transcend partisan lines, and is not very creative about problem solving. Prominent individuals have the ability to rise above factors that constrain typical politicians and generate new energy for the system as a whole.

But in other respects, a political system based on celebrity politics raises a host of troubling problems for democratic political systems. What we have done is develop a system where star power is weighted more heavily than traditional political skills such as bargaining, compromise, and experience. In earlier times, traditional politicians who rose through the ranks and who were skilled at compromise and conflict resolution were advantaged. The party system encouraged those types of individuals to enter politics and rewarded them through career advancement.

Now, these types of people have been replaced by another type of leader, namely those who are famous, media-savvy, and adept at fund-raising. In essence, our political system has substituted one type of leadership skills with another. The danger is that in this fundamental shift, important qualities such as experience, knowledge, and bargaining are de-emphasized, and that the system's ability to resolve conflict will suffer accordingly.

Celebrities are adept at raising issues and generating media attention, but tend toward more confrontational tactics. Less constrained by the need to negotiate with other people due to their star power and recognizing that conflict attracts press coverage, political newsworthies such as James Carville, John McCain, and Jesse Jackson often adopt polarizing tactics in order to push conventional politicians to take more substantial actions. These strategies are an excellent means for encouraging policy innovation, but not so helpful in terms of conflict resolution.

Given the types of qualities advantaged in our current system, there are some systemic problems that citizens should worry about. The following are among the features that are likely to persist in a system based on celebrity politics: expensive elections; news dramatizations that trivialize national news; gossip, rumor, and innuendo about major politicians; and a close integration of entertainment into our political process.

Expensive elections and costly lobbying battles mark our political system today.[3] Celebrities help to facilitate a spending arms race that advantages wealthy interests over grassroots groups. Because rich organizations have the best access to the rich and famous, a political system that revolves around celebrityhood advantages those at the top of the social and economic ladder, while disadvantaging other types of people.

The reliance on celebrity spokespeople elevates those of ascribed social status or those whose true achievements take place outside the political process. In recent years, both major parties have turned to the famous in order to focus attention on particular issues and to advance partisan interests. This puts celebrities into a special status and gives them disproportionate influence over our political system.

Our regime of celebrity politics makes it difficult to resolve emotional conflicts over pressing policy problems such as racism, sexism, AIDS, environmental destruction, homelessness, urban decay, and poverty. Given the current institutionalization of the celebrity political system as the dominant mode of American politics, it is difficult to determine whether our system will be able to address major national concerns. Too often, citizens are not given the material that would allow them to gain a better understanding of the complicated policy options we face. Rather than providing in-depth information, voters are given false choices, polarized options, and decisions framed by those who lack subject matter expertise.

In this kind of era, the media remain stuck in a tabloid universe. Scandal and background investigations continue to be the norm, and politicians face extensive scrutiny of their private lives. Many of the things that worry the general public—from reliance on anonymous sources to deceptive information-gathering techniques—continue to remain in the forefront for reporters. It is difficult in this situation for the media to chart a new course for itself.[4]

In short, celebrity politics accentuates many of the elements in our society that drain substance out of the political process and substitutes trivial and nonsubstantive forms of entertainment. Over the long run, this risks the short-circuiting of representative democracy and endangers the ability of ordinary citizens to hold leaders accountable for their policymaking decisions.

Unlikely political heroes do emerge for some people in the celebrity political system. Consider the international political superstardom of Nelson Mandela. This man rightfully became the dominant symbol of opposition to the brutal, racist apartheid system of government in South Africa when he was sentenced to life in 1962 for trying to organize a nationwide strike against apartheid in South Africa. By the early 1980s, "Free Mandela" signs began appearing on some U.S. campuses, and he became the symbol of struggle for the growing antiapartheid movement in the United States. Worldwide pressure, and domestic political pressure finally forced South Africa to release Nelson Mandela after twenty-seven years of prison in 1989.

This set the stage for the Nelson Mandela world tour. In the United States, he spent twelve days in eight cities and the events staged rivaled any rock star's tour. Mandela drew a huge crowd for his parade in New York, and he drew 50,000 people for a profit making rally at Yankee Stadium. Major celebrities like Spike Lee, Robert DeNiro, Joanne Woodward, and Eddie Murphy all threw fund-raisers for Mandela when he came to the United States. The media covered the event as the second coming of Dr. Martin Luther King, Jr. Mandela crossed over into the realm of being a superstar celebrity in America from his former role of dissident.[5]

Oliver North was another unlikely hero for some conservative Americans. Before he testified at the 1987 Iran-Contra investigations before the joint congressional committee, North was viewed by most Americans as a liar, a shredder of documents, a cover-up artist, a person who deceived Congress, and a potential criminal for his efforts to sell arms to Iran and give some of the profits to the Contras in Nicaragua in violation of the 1984 Boland amendment. North wore his military uniform for the first time since working for the National Security Council on his initial day of testimony. Even though he admitted lying, shredding documents, covering up, and deceiving Congress during the first day of testimony, North became a national folk hero to many Americans because of the way the media treated his testimony. He went on to run unsuccessfully for the U.S. Senate in Virginia, host his own radio talk show, and co-host a talk show on CNN.

Tom Brokaw of NBC announced to his audience after North first testified that his style and performance had been a grand slam home run, a touchdown, and a slam dunk. North's stylish admission of wrongdoing elevated him to superstar celebrity status. North kept his composure and argued with members of the committee about Central American foreign policy. He dominated arguments and came across to some as "Mr. Smith Goes to Washington." By the end of the televised testimony, "Olliemania" swept the country. There were Ollie dolls, T-shirts, haircuts, bumper stickers, books, and groupies. Now North is a celebrity who commands up to $30,000 per lecture as a hard-line conservative who argues that he was just a fall guy in the Iran-Contra investigation.[6]

Geraldine Ferraro is an example of a politician who became a political newsworthy and media figure. In 1984 when Ferraro was named by Walter Mondale to be the Democratic nominee for the vice presidency, she touched off a feminist celebration. Ferraro became a political celebrity and household name of the first magnitude. Then the media, who had promoted her almost as if she were heading the ticket, turned on her husband's financial situation. Media also focused on the anti-abortion protest to Ferraro's nomination because of her pro-choice position as a Catholic mother. Church clergy became famous for attacking Ferraro. Suddenly the conventional political wisdom deemed Ferraro to be a drag on the Democratic ticket. However, the conventional wisdom was wrong. Ferraro attracted larger political crowds than Mondale. She was the main celebrity attraction for the Democratic party.

After her defeat in 1984, the media kept up with Ferraro. Reporters covered the controversy over Ferraro's paid Pepsi commercial and of the continuing problems with her husband's business dealings. The media covered the arrest of her son, John Zaccaro, Jr., for selling cocaine while at school in Vermont. Yet Ferraro survived as a well-paid and popular lecture circuit speaker. She became a pundit on CNN and cohost of the popular show, *Crossfire*.

By 1992, she prepared to run for the U.S. Senate from New York. Ferraro was able to raise considerable money and attract extensive media attention. But in a crowded four-way field, she was unsuccessful in the effort.[7] She lost to fellow Democrat Robert Abrams, who then lost to incumbent Senator Al D'Amato.[8] She also lost another Senate bid to Charles Schumer in the 1998 Democratic primary. In each of these cases, celebrityhood allowed her to get her foot in the door, but not make the final sale with voters.

Such examples of celebrity heroes, however, may be more the exception than the rule. As discussed in Chapter 7, the contemporary media love to create celebrity "fools" who amuse the rest of us. President Gerald Ford was attacked in 1975 for being President "Bozo." The national news media focused on Ford's clumsiness and showed video of the president hitting a spectator with his golf ball, hitting his doubles partner on his serve while playing tennis, falling down stairs, hitting his head getting out of a helicopter and forgetting what state he was in. On NBC, *Saturday Night Live* and comedian Chevy Chase had a field day lampooning Ford. A series of Ford jokes swept the nation and serious presidential watchers talked about the "ridicule problem."

Vice presidents are easy targets for "fool" coverage. Vice President Spiro T. Agnew was turned into an American cartoonlike fool by forces in American popular culture. There were Agnew jokes, Agnew Mickey Mouse–type watches, and Agnew T-shirts that poked serious humor at Agnew.[9] Opponents even broadcast television ads laughing at his appearing on a national ticket. All of this occurred before Agnew was indicted on corruption charges stemming from his days as governor of Maryland.

Vice President Dan Quayle was lambasted even more than Agnew. A *Quayle Quarterly* was published nationally to keep citizens informed about the comings and goings of the clownish Quayle.

When he mistakenly added an "e" to the spelling of the word *potato*, it seemed to confirm all that was being said about the inexperienced vice president. Quayle jokes even continued after he finished his term. For years, Quayle jokes still popped up in Johnny Carson, Jay Leno, Arsenio Hall, and David Letterman monologues.

Some in the popular culture are able to overcome the "fool" label with extraordinary luck. President Ronald Reagan was the master of the one-liner, but he was also the master of the verbal gaffe.[10] His unbelievable misfires became part of the Reagan legend and part of his "teflon" ability to get away with things that other presidents could not.

Former president George Bush showed a similar propensity as Ronald Reagan for goofy statements, but Bush was treated by the mainstream press as some new macho warrior.[11] Only the late-night comedians picked on him for sentences that ended awkwardly and for his many idiosyncratic mannerisms. Bush's son, George W., also gets castigated for fractured language and obscure statements that cast doubt on his innate intelligence.

Still others get labeled as fools just because of media sensationalism. In 1987, the media worked on the assumption that it was the "Year of the Bimbo." In this instance, three different women, Fawn Hall, Donna Rice, and Jessica Hahn, became pop culture celebrities because of relationships with various male newsmakers.[12] Because they were female and attractive, it was easy for reporters to describe them in stereotypical language.

The pop culture celebrity system can make villains out of many people. Enemies of American presidents such as foreign leaders Moammar Khadafy, Slobodan Milosevic, and Saddam Hussein become pop culture villains in the United States as the American media takes White House, State Department, and Department of Defense press handouts and broadcasts them virtually verbatim. It is far easier to conduct foreign policy when particular opponents are demonized and caricaturized in unfavorable ways.

Over the past decades, mass media has institutionalized gossip stories to make national villains out of domestic politicians because of happenings in their private lives. For example, Gary Hart, Joe Biden, Barney Frank, John Tower, and others were investigated by the press, and intimate secrets were reported about their personal conduct. This forced people out of presidential campaigns and denied positions in government to others.

In the celebrity political system, respected stars are often treated as great intellectuals and oracles for society.[13] Just because they are entertainment figures with a huge following, interviewers often ask them about the state of world peace, their position on the Middle East, the environment, presidential politics, and so on. This trend to treat celebrities with an unusual amount of deference in public debate has led to an unusual celebrity political system where stars have become major politicos.

But now it seems that celebrities have crossed over into a new political activism. Richard Bernstein asked the correct question, "Should stars set the agenda?"[14] This book has argued that they clearly should not be setting the American political agenda. Most entertainment figures do not have the training, background, or experience to offer much other than opinions about important national and international events. Yet, even those leaders and media commentators who have the ability to set the national agenda are treated as newsworthy figures.

Celebrities have learned to pick and choose their causes carefully. During the Iraq War in 1991, major celebrities whom one would have thought might have been outspoken in antiwar opposition, recognized the overwhelming national support that had been manufactured by President Bush. As Judith

Michaelson and Diane Haithman noted, it was "All Quiet on the Hollywood Front."[15] Celebrities joined forces to record a song called "Voices That Care" to show their support for the troops in the Iraq War. Among the celebrities who wanted to be on record as supporting American troops were Meryl Streep, Kevin Costner, Bette Midler, Whoopi Goldberg, and Vanna White.[16]

Rock music, which during the Vietnam War era was considered antiwar, antigovernment, and perhaps antiestablishment, fit right into the war. The rock group Van Halen was proud that U.S. bomber pilots liked to listen to Van Halen albums when carrying out strikes against Iraq.[17] Other troops reported that they enjoyed carrying out their duties to the music of the Rolling Stones' "Satisfaction" or Bob Dylan's "Hard Rain's A Gonna Fall."[18]

When one celebrity, Margot Kidder, stepped out of line from the American consensus in favor of the war, she was quickly criticized by opponents. Kidder appeared at an antiwar rally in New York and said, "Saddam Hussein is a monster, but may I remind you that the ultimate human-rights abuse is war."[19] Later, in response to Hussein's possible mistreatment of American bomber pilots who had become prisoners of war after they were shot down over Iraq, Kidder said, "Here are the boys' rules of war. You're allowed to go in and bomb . . . and kill God knows how many people . . . but you're not allowed to ridicule an American soldier who is caught. Give me a break."[20] After the ensuing media firestorm over her remarks, Kidder had to take a low profile as some tried to portray her as the Jane Fonda of the 1990s. The real Jane Fonda had no comment. Kidder finally had to issue a statement saying she supported the American troops and that she wanted them to return home safely.

While Americans continue to *watch* politics happen, citizens must get ready for the next round of presidential games to follow. What celebrities will endorse which Republican or Democratic candidate for the next presidency? What celebrities will *become* Republican or Democratic candidates? In 2000, actor Warren Beatty briefly toyed with the idea of running for president. In the future, perhaps Bruce Springsteen, Phil Donahue, Michael Jordan, Charles Barkley, or Jackson Browne may well run for elective office.

Celebrity has become a product of our contemporary society. It has been manufactured by a process and it is used to sell all kinds of products. As Deyan Sudjic noted a decade ago, "Celebrity will undoubtedly be the greatest growth industry of the 1990s."[21] Celebrities from one area often cross over into other areas almost as if their celebrityhood were transferable. Some sports celebrities dabble in television, advertising, show business, and rock music, for example. Rock stars try their wares in movies, television talk shows, situation comedies, and in celebrity sporting events. Some movie stars play at rock, sport, and comedy. It is when the celebrities from the entertainment world cross over into the political system, and when the celebrities from the world of politics cross over into the world of entertainment, that the celebrity political system is generated.

Television presents the images of the celebrity to the mass audience. The images come at viewers with blinding speed. Citizens celebrate the short time that the celebrity is prominent in the media and then the image fades. Attention spans for serious political crises, issues and gossip and scandal are all merged together for a short, two-day or three-day attention span during the cycled representation of celebrities.

Celebrities become products and are endowed with expertise outside of their celebrated area. For example, sometimes home run hitters are asked about their solutions to apartheid in South Africa. Rock stars are asked to explain their environmental record as if they were running for office. Movie stars are queried about their lifestyle choices and their stands on sexual preferences. Comedians are asked to give political commentary and television stars are asked about animal rights. Serious political issues become trivialized in this attempt to elevate celebrities to philosopher-celebrities.

The celebrity political culture is transmitted to citizens by television, yet the electronic medium has a strange sense of time and history. Television's memory is that memory which can be recalled by video clips or talking heads. As Patricia Mellencamp has observed, "TV memories of TV is an endless chain of TV referentials."[22] There is no connection between news items or celebrity representations. It is all nondifferentiated television entertainment.

By being on television in what Herbert Zettl calls "first-order space" and shot with customary, very intimate close-ups, celebrities may become as a real person to citizens rather than as a television image.[23] Media celebrities take the place of old-fashioned heroes and role models. A celebrity is followed and noted rather than honored for any specific moral stands. The ease at which some people become celebrities in the political system is based on luck, fortune, and timing, but not necessarily talent. With television's emphasis on the visual, the celebrity system is geared toward the look, and the image. There becomes a perceived "community of celebrities." Citizens become fans who, by some accounts, try to live vicariously through the lives of the well known celebrity.[24]

Yet in a celebrity regime, fans can have power. Ordinary people decide what images will last and which celebrities will be of lasting importance. Fans are the economic consumers of the entertainment provided by celebrityhood.[25] Citizens can take back the power in the current celebrity political system, and say no to the system that features politicians as celebrities, celebrities as politicians, celebrities as endorsers, and celebrities as social activists. Voters can do this by discerning which features of celebrity politics are unproductive and protecting themselves accordingly.

In the future, it will be necessary for citizens to discriminate and evaluate celebrity images that bombard them. Citizens can decide which celebrities will be taken seriously and which celebrities will be allowed to cross over into other areas in which they have yet to show talent. Merely being famous should not be grounds for gaining a prominent role in national political discussions.

Citizens can demand a political journalism that seeks to inform rather than titillate and a public discourse that illuminates rather than trivializes politics. Democratic political systems require in-depth information so that citizens can judge leaders and hold them accountable. Sadly, the contemporary period does not provide the quality of material that citizens need in order to make informed choices.

If we don't take back the celebrity political system, citizens might well face a political contest between a basketball player versus a football player, or a comedian versus a rock star, or a movie star versus a television situation comedy star. Elections are the key vehicle by which representative democracy takes place. Unless citizens receive proper information and candidates provide meaningful choices, it short-circuits the democratic procedures that all Americans value. We all deserve better choices than that currently provided in our regime based on celebrity politics.

NOTES

1. Orrin Klapp, *Heroes, Villains and Fools: The Changing American Character* (Englewood Cliffs, NJ: Prentice Hall, 1972).
2. Burton Hersh, *The Education of Edward Kennedy* (New York: Morrow, 1972).
3. Darrell West and Burdett Loomis, *The Sound of Money* (New York: Norton, 1998).
4. Darrell M. West, *The Rise and Fall of the Media Establishment* (Boston: Bedford/St. Martin's Press, 2001).
5. Richard Lacayo, "A Hero in America," *Time*, 2 July 1990.
6. Thomas DeFrank, "Ollie North's Road Show," *Newsweek*, August 1988, p. 24.
7. James Adams, "The Lost Honor of Geraldine Ferraro," *Commentary* 81 (February 1986), pp. 34–38.
8. Marc Humbert, "Geraldine Ferraro Reportedly Will Challenge D'Amato for Senate in New York," Associated Press, 1998. Reported on Nando.net Web site.
9. Henry Beck, "Spiro Agnew the Fool." Paper presented to the American Political Science Association Annual Meetings, September 3, 1977 and Ken Sokolow, "Spiro T. Agnew Trivia Contest," *Baltimore Magazine*, October 1983, p. 74.
10. Morton Mintz and Margaret Mintz, eds., *Quotations from President Ron* (London: MacDonald and Company, 1987).
11. Ken Brady and Jeremy Solomon, *The Wit and Wisdom of George Bush* (New York: St. Martin's, 1989).
12. "The Year of the Bimbo," *New Republic*, 4 January 1988, p. 10.
13. Mary Harron, "McRock," in *Facing the Music*, ed. Simon Frith (New York: Pantheon Books, 1988), p. 189.
14. Richard Bernstein, "Should Stars Set the Agenda?" *New York Times*, 10 March 1991, pp. 11 and 18ff.
15. Judith Michaelson and Diane Haithman, "All Quiet on the Hollywood Front," *Los Angeles Times*, 17 February 1991, Calendar, pp. 6 and 58ff.
16. Edna Gunderson, "Celebs Sing Out in Support of Soldiers," *USA Today*, 30 January 1991, p. D-1 and Janice Simpson, "Good Morning, Saudi Arabia," *Time*, 4 March 1991, p. 72.

17. Edna Gunderson, "Rock's Roar Soars over the Gulf War," *USA Today*, 28 January 1991, p. 2-D.

18. Judy Keen, "'Satisfaction' 'Bartman' 'Pump Up the Troops,'" *USA Today*, 28 January 1991, p. 2-D.

19. Kitty Bean Yancey, "Kidder's Remarks on War Draw Fire," *USA Today*, 23 January 1991, p. 2-D.

20. Kitty Bean Yancey, "Kidder's Remarks on War Draw Fire," *USA Today*, 23 January 1991, p. 2-D.

21. Deyan Sudjic, *Cult Heroes: How to Be Famous for More Than Fifteen Minutes* (London: Andre Deutsch Limited, 1989), p. 15.

22. Patricia Mellencamp, "TV Times and Catastrophe" in *Logics of Television*, ed. Patricia Mellencamp (Bloomington, IN: Indiana University Press, 1990), p. 242.

23. Herbert Zettl, "The Graphication and Personification of Television News" in *Television Studies: Textual Analysis*, ed. Gary Burns and Robert J. Thompson (New York: Praeger, 1989), p. 157.

24. Richard Schickel, *Intimate Strangers: The Culture of Celebrity* (Garden City, NY: Doubleday, 1985).

25. See Lisa A. Lewis, ed., *The Adoring Audience: Fan Culture and Popular Media* (London and New York: Routledge, 1992) for a positive look at the power of fans.

INDEX